Study Guide

for

Elmes, Kantowitz, and Roediger's

Research Methods in Psychology

Study Guide

for

Elmes, Kantowitz, and Roediger's

Research Methods in Psychology
Eighth Edition

Chris Koch
George Fox University

Michael D. Hall
James Madison University

THOMSON
™
WADSWORTH

Australia • Brazil • Canada • Mexico • Singapore • Spain • United Kingdom • United States

Printed in the United States of America

1 2 3 4 5 6 7   09 08 07 06 05

Printer: EPAC Technologies, Inc.

ISBN 0-534-60977-5

Cover Image: W. Cody/Corbis

Thomson Higher Education
10 Davis Drive
Belmont, CA 94002-3098
USA

For more information about our products, contact us at:
Thomson Learning Academic Resource Center
1-800-423-0563

For permission to use material from this text or product, submit a request online at **http://www.thomsonrights.com**.
Any additional questions about permissions can be submitted by email to **thomsonrights@thomson.com**.

We would like to thank Joseph B. Thompson, Washington and Lee University, and Wayne G. Brake for their work on previous editions of this study guide.

The current edition has several features to assist the student with both memorizing and, more importantly, understanding concepts outlined in the main text by Elmes, Kantowitz and Roediger.

As in the seventh edition, this edition has chapter outlines, lists of definitions of the key words for each chapter (*Learning the Terminology*), along with fill-in-the-blank, multiple choice, and true-false questions.

All chapters now have *Experimental Dilemmas* to help apply concepts in the main text to real research scenarios. Additional *Web Resources* and *Further Readings* have been provided for each chapter as well. Finally, online tutorials from the Research Methods Workshop for various topics covered in the text are noted in appropriate chapters.

Enjoy the course and learning about the science of psychology.

Christopher Koch, Ph.D.
George Fox University

Michael D. Hall, Ph.D.
James Madison University

CONTENTS

Chapter 1

Overview of Psychological Research

SUMMARY
1. Goals of Psychological Research
   1.1. Conducting Research
       1.1.1.   science progresses when new facts lead to new theories
       1.1.2.   scientific progress is driven by basic questions about theories and practical problems
   1.2. Evaluating Research
       1.2.1.   a **critical thinker** exercises careful judgment
       1.2.2.   in an ideal experiment
           1.2.2.1. something is manipulated (**independent variable**)
           1.2.2.2. behavior is measured (**dependent variable**)
           1.2.2.3. potential sources of influence are held constant (**control variables**)
       1.2.3.   **confounding** occurs when a factor(s) in addition to the independent variable change in a study
           1.2.3.1. confounding is a threat to **internal validity** or the ability to attribute the cause of behavioral change to the independent variable
           1.2.3.2. confounding is an important consideration for a critical thinker
2. Typical Steps in Research
   2.1. Get an idea
   2.2. Formulate a testable hypothesis
   2.3. Review the literature
   2.4. Conduct a pilot study
   2.5. Complete the research
   2.6. Conduct statistical tests
   2.7. Interpret the results
   2.8. Prepare an article
3. Sources of Research Ideas
   3.1. Observation – observing one's own behavior, the behavior of others (including animals), and particular situations can generate research questions
   3.2. Experts – can be a source of research ideas and can provide important feedback on the questions you generate on your own
   3.3. Literature Search – journal articles, chapters, and books are sources of research ideas
       3.3.1.   maintain a list of research ideas as you read journal articles and books
           3.3.1.1. record the reference information with the research idea so you remember the source of the idea

        3.3.2.   *PsycINFO* is an electronic database to search for references in psychology

4. Developing Testable Hypotheses
   - 4.1. a **testable hypothesis** specifies a relationship between two or more variables
     - 4.1.1. implies that the variables are measurable (and observable)
     - 4.1.2. specifies a relationship
   - 4.2. since scientific research requires variables to be observed and measured, if a hypothesis is not testable then it cannot be examined scientifically
   - 4.3. not all hypotheses can be examined through research

5. Reviewing the Literature
   - 5.1. explore the literature to determine what is known about your hypothesis
   - 5.2. citations in textbooks can be a starting point
   - 5.3. reference lists from books and journal articles can be a valuable source of relevant articles
   - 5.4. review articles are excellent sources of information

6. Conducting Pilot Research
   - 6.1. **pilot research** is preliminary research in which you test a small number of participants to make sure that your study runs smoothly
     - 6.1.1. helps determine if participants understand the instructions
     - 6.1.2. helps determine how long the study takes
     - 6.1.3. see if the task is too easy or too difficult
     - 6.1.4. provides practice using the equipment, administering tests, and making observations
   - 6.2. one goal of pilot research is to determine if the appropriate levels of the independent variable are being used to have the desired effect on the dependent variable

7. Some Pitfalls to Avoid
   - 7.1. breaches of ethical practice
     - 7.1.1. human research
       - 7.1.1.1. maintain the well-being of the participants by treating them as you would like to be treated
       - 7.1.1.2. avoid or minimize physical or mental harm
       - 7.1.1.3. maintain confidentiality
       - 7.1.1.4. avoid deception and dishonesty
     - 7.1.2. animal research
       - 7.1.2.1. must treat animals humanely
       - 7.1.2.2. research cannot lead to cruelty or negligent treatment
       - 7.1.2.3. organizations such as the APA have guidelines for animal research
       - 7.1.2.4. federal and state agencies also regulate animal research
   - 7.2. biased research
     - 7.2.1. deliberate fraud, or purposively providing false results, is uncommon
     - 7.2.2. **inadvertent researcher bias** results from a variety of sources reflecting the attitudes and preferences of the researcher
       - 7.2.2.1. researchers should be aware of their preconceptions and

7.2.2.2. use several different strategies to study a problem in order to minimize inadvertent researcher bias
7.2.3. all participants should be treated the same way in the study
    7.2.3.1. **protocols** are lists of procedures and methods used to test participants in a given study
        7.2.3.1.1. following a protocol (or script) helps ensure that all participants are treated in the same way
    7.2.3.2. making a researcher blind to an important characteristic of the participants or the task keeps him or her from treating participants in a manner biased in the direction of the hypothesis
        7.2.3.2.1. in a **double-blind design,** both the participant and researcher are blind to the treatment conditions
        7.2.3.2.2. a **placebo** is an inert substance received by the control group
            7.2.3.2.2.1. the participants believe they are receiving the active drug
            7.2.3.2.2.2. the research does not know which participants receive the placebo (this information in maintained someone else)
7.2.4. **anthropomorphizing,** or the assigning of human characteristics to animals, is a potential problem when interpreting findings in animal research
7.3. reliability of communication
    7.3.1. technical usage of terms is more stringent or precise than common usage
    7.3.2. **operational definitions** provide exact definitions of how something is measured
        7.3.2.1. procedures or operations for measurement are specified
        7.3.2.2. **reliability** refers to how consistently a measurement can be obtained
8. Finishing the Research Project
    8.1. after completing a research project, it is important to communicate the results to others in a written paper

LEARNING THE TERMINOLOGY

Anthropomorphizing. Attributing human characteristics or emotions, such as happiness, to animals (p.20). Thinking your cat wants affection when it really seeks your body heat

Behavior. The basic dependent variable of psychology (p. 3). Examining memory by measuring the ability to recall a list of words. The ability to recall words is the behavior.

Blind Experiment. That in which participants do not know whether they are in the treatment or control condition (p. 19). Giving some participants a drug and others a placebo, but not telling them which they are receiving.

Confounding. Simultaneous variation of some uncontrolled variable with the independent variable (p. 9). The idea that participants in an experiment will get bored toward the end of the experiment and perform more poorly on those tasks even though the tasks aren't harder.

Control Variable. A potential independent variable that is held constant in an experiment (p. 7). See placebo.

Critic. A person who makes an informed judgment (p. 7). A person who weighs their evaluation of research findings based upon reading the primary literature and carefully examining whether the research was well conducted.

Critical Thinker. A person who approaches scientific procedures and results with a critical attitude (p. 7). See critic above.

Dependent Variable. The variable measured and recorded by the researcher (p. 7). This is typically some behavior in psychology such as aggression in boys during play.

Double Blind Design. Experimental technique in which neither the participant nor the experimenter knows which participants are in which treatment condition (p. 19). When testing the effects of a new drug, neither the participants nor the experimenter who is measuring their behavior knows which drug the participants have been given.

Ethical Issues. Issues that underscore the importance of ensuring the well being of human or animal subjects in an experiment (p. 17). Making sure not to cause emotional distress to participants in an experiment.

Inadvertent Researcher Bias. Unplanned bias owing to the characteristics of the researcher (p. 17). A researcher expects that males will be better at math than females and, without intending to, scores the math quizzes taken by males more generously than those taken by females, biasing the findings.

Independent Variable. The variable manipulated by the experimenter (p. 7). Testing whether attitude affects ability to learn a second language, a researcher would test participants with positive attitudes versus negative attitudes on the ability to learn. The selection of participants with either positive or negative attitudes is the independent variable.

Internal Validity. Refers to the degree to which causal statements about the relationship between variables can be made (p. 10).

Operational Definition. A definition of a concept in terms of the operations that must be performed to demonstrate the concept (p. 21). Providing a scale outlining exactly how violence is measured for a study on T.V. violence.

4

Pilot Research. Preliminary research undertaken to discover problems of method and design for a subsequent full-scale project (p. 16). Testing a few subjects for a later experiment on math ability to see how much time is needed to finish the math quizzes and whether the quizzes are too difficult.

Placebo. A physiologically inert substance (p. 19). A sugar pill given to participants to deceive them into thinking they may be receiving a drug.

Protocol. A recipe to be followed exactly in conducting a research project (p. 18) A description detailing how the research is to be carried out, including how long participants should wait between tests, what time of day they are tested, and what should be said to them during the experiment.

Reliability. Refers to the relative consistency of behavioral measures (p. 21).

Testable Hypothesis. A hypothesis that specifies what can be measured or manipulated to test a theory (p. 13). A hypothesis stating that T.V. violence is responsible for problems in society is NOT testable. A hypothesis that T.V. violence increases aggression during play behavior in children IS a testable hypothesis.

KEY TERM MATCHING

1.	
___anthropomorphizing ___confounding ___inadvertent researcher bias ___placebo ___testable hypothesis	a. Allowing an uncontrolled variable to change together with changes in the independent variable. b. Attributing human characteristics to animals. c. Influences on the research by expectations of the data collector. d. A research idea that can be reasonably answered. e. A variable that is held constant in an experiment. f. A pharmacologically inert substance.
2.	
___dependent variable ___independent variable ___critical thinker ___protocol	a. What the experimenter manipulates. b. A control for researcher bias. c. A recipe for conducting research. d. One who makes informed and reasoned judgments. e. What the experimenter observes or measures.

3.	a. A control for researcher bias.
___double blind design	b. A way to reduce ambiguous communication.
	c. A means of dealing with an ethical issue.
___control variable	d. Useful in determining whether an experiment will work
___pilot research	e. A statement of the relationship between two variables.
___treating animals humanely	f. A variable that remains constant.
___operational definition	

FILL IN THE BLANK

1. _____ refers to observable activities of people and animals.
2. Psychologists often conduct research for two basic reasons: To develop theoretical _____ of a behavior of interest, and to solve _____.
3. A _____ is a person who makes an informed or reasoned judgment about the value of information.
4. In an experiment, the _____ _____ is deliberately manipulated to determine its effect on behavior.
5. The _____ _____ is the aspect of behavior that is measured in a psychology experiment.
6. _____ _____ are held constant so that they will not inadvertently influence the behavior of interest in an experiment.
7. _____ occurs when a variable not of interest happens to change together with changes in the independent variable.
8. Science begins with _____ -both as a source of data and as a source for research ideas.
9. Professors and other _____ may suggest research projects, or help you refine your own research ideas.
10. _____ and _____ _____ are good general resources that will help you find journal articles relevant to your research ideas.
11. After you have identified a problem or idea to investigate, the next step is to formulate a _____ _____.
12. Hypotheses will not be testable unless they include variables that are _____ and specify _____ among variables.
13. In addition to suggesting ideas, a _____ _____ will help you discover what is already known about your hypothesis.
14. Another name for preliminary research is _____ research.
15. An _____ _____ is a formula for building a construct in a way that other scientists can duplicate.

MULTIPLE CHOICE

1. Which of the following NOT a form of behavior that psychologists measure
   a. recalling a story.
   b. observable overt activities of people and animals.
   c. physiological indicators of thoughts and feelings.
   d. all of the above can be measured.

2. Practical gains from psychological research include
   a. improved methods of treating psychologically disordered people.
   b. new ways of making workers happy and performing better.
   c. improving the design of cars to make them safer.
   d. all of the above

3. In the demonstration experiment on reading and counting, the fastest condition was
   a. reading digits.
   b. counting +'s.
   c. counting digits.
   d. there were no differences among these conditions.

4. In the demonstration experiment on reading and counting, the slowest condition was
   a. reading digits.
   b. counting +'s.
   c. counting digits.
   d. there were no differences among these conditions.

5. Experimental psychologists engage in research
   a. to make money.
   b. to solve practical problems.
   c. because their professor requires it.
   d. to develop a subjective understanding of some phenomenon.

6. A critic
   a. makes informed or reasoned judgments.
   b. finds fault with the work of others.
   c. is less objective than an evaluator.
   d. is one who is unable to engage in research directly.

7. In an experiment, the independent variable is
   a. measured by the experimenter.
   b. manipulated by the experimenter.
   c. held constant.
   d. is confounding.

8. In an experiment, the dependent variable is
   a. measured by the experimenter.
   b. manipulated by the experimenter.
   c. held constant.
   d. is confounding.

9. In an experiment, a control variable is
   a. measured by the experimenter.
   b. manipulated by the experimenter.
   c. held constant.
   d. is confounding.

10. When some aspect of an experiment changes along with changes in the independent variable,
    a. you are more likely to get interpretable results.
    b. you are more likely to get large behavioral effects.
    c. your experiment had control.
    d. confounding has occurred.

11. In the demonstration experiment of the Stroop effect, what was confounded with the levels of the independent variable?
    a. response time
    b. task differences
    c. response ordering
    d. task ordering

12. Research ideas can come from
    a. consulting with an expert.
    b. reading journal articles.
    c. identifying practical problems.
    d. all of the above

13. A statement about a presumed or theoretical relationship between two or more variables that includes a description of how these variables are to be measured is called a
    a. psychological theory.
    b. testable hypothesis.
    c. citation abstract.
    d. research design.

14. In addition to providing research ideas, a literature search is useful in
    a. finding out if your research hypothesis has already been studied.
    b. finding out if your hypothesis is true.
    c. providing your results
    d. providing control in your experiment

15. Preliminary research performed before beginning a full-scale experiment
    a. is called pilot research.
    b. allows you to get the bugs out of your experimental procedure.
    c. allows you to identify useful levels of your independent variable.
    d. all of the above

TRUE FALSE

1. There is no reason to learn about research, unless you personally plan to conduct research.

2. It is possible for research findings to be useful, even if they don't increase our theoretical understanding.

3. If confounding has occurred, the effect of the independent variable is always overestimated.

4. How the researcher treats the participants can have an effect on the results of an experiment.

5. *PsycINFO* is the only source for finding titles of articles from journals that publish psychological research.

6. If the variables mentioned in a hypothesis are not measurable, the hypothesis is not testable.

EXPERIMENTAL DILEMMAS

(I) A counseling psychologist believes that physical exercise will help patients suffering from chronic depression. The psychologist is currently treating 39 people who are suffering from chronic depression. Thirty-six of these people said that they would be willing to participate in an experiment if the experiment might help them and might also provide information that would help the psychologist to learn more about how to help depressed people.

The psychologist administered a standard paper and pencil test to measure how depressed his subjects were before treatment. The psychologist used these scores to match 12 groups of three people who scored about the same on the depression test. These three people were then randomly assigned to treatment conditions.

People in condition 1 were then asked to engage in some sort of outdoors exercise three times a week, people in condition 2 exercised five times a week, and people in condition 3 were not asked to exercise, but they were asked to spend some time outdoors at least three times a week.

At the end of the six-week experiment the subjects took another paper and pencil depression test. The results showed that all subjects were now rated as less depressed than they were at the beginning of the experiment. However, the subjects in conditions 1 and 2 had improved more than the subjects in condition 3. Subjects in conditions 1 and 2 had improved the same amount over the six-week period.

The psychologist concluded that exercise provides help above and beyond that provided by simply spending time outdoors. He also concluded that three days of exercise a week was enough to benefit the depressed person.

1) What was the hypothesis tested by the researcher?

2) What were the independent and dependent variables?

3) What did the experimenter attempt to control in this study? How was this control achieved?

(II) A cognitive psychologist wishes to examine the effects of signaling in multimedia. The theory behind the research is that signaling makes key ideas and relationships more explicit and easier to process. For example when key words are underlined or in **bold** in a written passage, the reader will more likely remember and understand the passage.

The cognitive psychologist is working for a website design company and wishes to test the idea that other types of signaling such as flashing words or text in different colors is also important for web based information processing.

1) What could be a testable hypothesis by the researcher above?
2) Provide an operational definition that could be used in an experiment above.
3) How could the researcher avoid bias in this study?
4) There are many different careers in psychology, can you think of other ways psychologists can work with internet companies?

ANSWER KEY

Key Term Matching
1. b, a, c, f, d
2. e, a, c, f, d
3. a, f, d, c, b

Fill in the Blank
1. behavior (p. 3)
2. understanding, practical problems (p. 6)
3. critic (p. 7)
4. independent variable (p. 7)
5. dependent variable (p. 7)
6. control variables (p. 7)
7. confounding (p. 9)
8. observation (p. 11)
9. experts (p. 11)
10. *PsycINFO, Psychological Abstracts* (p. 13)
11. testable hypothesis (p. 13)
12. measurable, relationships (p. 13)
13. literature search (p. 14)
14. pilot (p. 16)
15. operational definition (p. 21)

Multiple Choice
1. d (p. 3)
2. d (p. 3)
3. a (p. 5)
4. c (p. 5)
5. b (p. 8)
6. a (p. 7)
7. b (p. 7)
8. a (p. 7)
9. c (p. 7)
10. d (p. 9)
11. d (p. 25)
12. d (p. 11)
13. b (p. 13)
14. a (p. 12)
15. d (p. 16)

True or False
1. F (p. 8)
2. T (p. 6)
3. F (p. 10)
4. T (p. 18)
5. F (p. 13)
6. T (p. 13)

Experimental Dilemmas

(I)

1) An example hypothesis might be: "Physical exercise alleviates symptoms of chronic depression."
2) The independent variable was: amount of exercise (no exercise, 3 times a week, or 5 times a week). The dependent variable was degree of depression (measured by paper and pencil depression test).
3) The experimenter tried to control two things: 1) differences in level of depression of the participants 2) as well as whether simply being outside will improve depression. The psychologist tested subjects before the experiment began (to make sure one group was not more depressed than another at the outset by matching participants) and had subjects who were not exercising spend time outdoors to control for the fact that those exercising will also be getting out of the house and exposed to sunlight and nature etc...

(II)

1) Signaling such as flashing words or different color words will increase understanding and memorization of the information/content contained in websites.
2) There could be multiple answers to this question. Basically, the researcher would have to define exactly how he/she was measuring both understanding and memorization. One example of an operational definition for memorization might be the number of facts recalled from the total number of facts contained in a website that participants read. An example of an operational definition for understanding could be the number of correct answers from a defined list of questions whose answers require implicit understanding of the information on the website.
3) The researcher could avoid bias by using a double blind design. The participants would not know whether memory of, or understanding of, the passage they were reading was enhanced by signals (such as flashing words or different colors) and the researcher would not know which participants read which type of passage when scoring their recall and understanding tests. Note that participants would obviously know whether there were flashing words etc on their website, but they would not know that it was an important component of the experiment in a double blind study.
4) The possibilities are numerous and increasing daily. One example is to be hired to examine whether people would be more likely to purchase products on a website based upon its content. Another would be to help design websites that are more user friendly. There are many psychologists currently employed in the dot.com industry doing just those types of things! These types of careers may be considered a branch of *industrial* or *applied* psychology.

FURTHER READINGS

For those students wishing to learn about current debates in psychology research the following is an example...

Strickland, B.R. (2000). Misassumptions, misadventures, and the misuse of psychology. *American Psychologist, 55*, 331-338.

For those who wish to learn more about how psychology got started as a science....

Sokal, M.M. (1998). On history of psychology's launch. *History of Psychology, 1*, 3-7.

Sokal, M. M, Davis, A. B, & Merzbach, U. C. (1976). Laboratory instruments in the history of psychology. *Journal of the History of the Behavioral Sciences, 12*, 59-64.

WEB RESOURCES

An interesting site to accompany the Sokal, Davis, and Merzbach (1976) article on instruments used in psychological research is the Psychology Instruments Museum at the University of Toronto (http://psych.utoronto.ca/museum/). You can also find information about research devices at the Archives of the History of American Psychology (http://www3.uakron.edu/ahap/apparatus/categories.phtml).

Summary information concerning theories and phases of research can be found at the Cyberlab website (http://faculty.frostburg.edu/mbradley/cyberlab.htm) maintained by Dr. Megan E. Bradley.

RESEARCH METHODS WORKSHOPS

Getting Ideas for a Study is a workshop that helps you determine potential sources of research ideas. Two important topics are presented in Chapter 1. These include confounds and constructs. There are workshops for each of these topics (*Confounds-Threats to Validity, Specifying Constructs*, and *Operational Definitions*). Wadsworth's Research Methods Workshops can be found at: http://psychology.wadsworth.com/workshops/.

Chapter 2

Explanation in Scientific Psychology

SUMMARY
1. Sources of Understanding
   1.1. non-scientific ways of knowing (Charles Sanders Peirce, 1877)
      1.1.1. **method of authority** – belief held by taking someone else's word for it
      1.1.2. **method of tenacity** – refuse to alter knowledge or opinion in spite of contradictory evidence
      1.1.3. **a priori** – beliefs held because they seem reasonable
   1.2. **scientific method** – beliefs based on experience and characterized by the following features
      1.2.1. **empirical** – based on experience or what is observable
      1.2.2. **repeatable** – replication of findings increases confidence in those findings
      1.2.3. **self-correcting** – new ideas can be compared with old ideas so that incorrect ideas can be discarded
2. The Nature of Scientific Explanation
      2.1.1. **basic elements of science**
         2.1.1.1. data are obtained from empirical observation
         2.1.1.2. theories organize concepts and allow for prediction of data
      2.1.2. **induction** –data leads to theory
         2.1.2.1. one problem is that data are linked to the circumstances under which they were observed making theories resulting from data tentative since collected data under difference circumstances could produce a different theory
      2.1.3. **deduction** – theory predicts data
         2.1.3.1. good theories must be testable and the tests must be able to show if empirical predictions are false (**falsifiability view**)
         2.1.3.2. one problem is that theories are often made with certain assumptions and if these assumptions are false then the theories are faulty as well
      2.1.4. induction and deduction exist in a circular relationship to yield scientific understanding
         2.1.4.1. **strong inference** is an eliminative procedure in which two possibilities are compared to determine which one is empirically supported
3. From Theory to Hypothesis
   3.1. hypothesis versus generalizations
      3.1.1. **hypothesis** – testable statement evaluated with data
         3.1.1.1. common-sense hypotheses are inductively derived from data

3.1.1.2. most hypotheses are deductively derived from theories

   3.1.2. **generalization** – broad statement not directly testable

   3.1.3. a good theory produces many generalizations each of which produce a number of hypotheses

4. What is a Theory?

  4.1. a theory is a set a statements that <u>organizes</u> existing data and makes <u>predictions</u> about future data

    4.1.1. **organization** and **prediction** are the two major functions of a theory (sometimes referred to as description and explanation respectively)

    4.1.2. generally, the more data a theory is able to explain with the relatively few statements the better the theory (**parsimony**)

  4.2. intervening variables

    4.2.1. independent variable is manipulated in a study to examine changes in behavior

    4.2.2. dependent variables are measured behaviors

    4.2.3. **intervening variables** are abstract concepts that link independent and dependent variables together

  4.3. three criteria for evaluating theories

    4.3.1. **parsimony** (Occam's razor) – the more economical a theory is in regard to number of statements and the more data it actually predicts the more parsimonious it is

    4.3.2. **precision** – predictions need to be precise enough so that different researchers can agree on the predictions

    4.3.3. **testability** – must be testable (refer to falsifiability view)

5. The Science of Psychology

  5.1. hard science as a model for experimental psychology – all sciences have data and theories

  5.2. psychology and the real world

    5.2.1. **basic research** is focused on data collection and theory development

    5.2.2. **applied research** is directly at a practical problem with an immediate application

LEARNING THE TERMINOLOGY

Applied research. Research whose focus is on solving a practical problem (p. 50). Research aimed at increasing worker productivity.

A priori method. According to Pierce, a way of fixing belief due to the reasonableness of the event (see method of tenacity, method of authority, and empirical) (p. 33). Assuming that women are more emotional than men before ever conducting experiments to determine if it is so.

Basic research. Research in which the focus is on understanding rather than on the immediate solution to a problem (p. 50). A scientist who studies the organization of the retina involved in processing visual information.

Data. The scores obtained on a dependent variable (p. 34). The information a psychologist collects from observation ; such as scores on a math quiz.

Deduction. Reasoning from the general to the particular (p. 35). Developing a theory on post-traumatic stress disorder , and then testing patients to see if this theory holds true.

Diffusion of responsibility. The tendency for individuals to assume less responsibility to act in a group situation (p. 31). When people work alone they feel responsible for the completing the task whereas in a group they feel less responsible.

Empirical. Relying on or derived from observation or experiment (p. 33). Believing the world is round based on experimentation rather than it being flat based on faith.

Falsifiability view. The assertion by Popper that negative results are more informative than positive results (p. 37). Conducting experiments aimed at disproving a theory rather than confirming it.

Generalization. A broad statement derived from a theory that cannot be tested directly (p. 39). Generalizing that older drivers are unsafe at any speed and should have driving restrictions.

Hypothesis. A very specific testable statement derived from a theory that can be evaluated from observable data (p. 39). Drivers older than 65 years would have a higher frequency of accidents involving left turns across on-coming traffic when driving at night than younger drivers.

Induction. Reasoning from the particular to the general (p. 35). Developing a theory on post-traumatic stress disorder based upon many observations on these patients.

Intervening variable. An abstract concept that links independent variables to dependent variables (p. 43). Addiction maybe an intervening variable to explain why prior drug use increases future drug use.

Method of authority. A method of fixing belief in which an authority's word is taken on faith; contrast with empirical (p. 32). Believing these definitions simply because they are in a textbook and your professor says they are true.

Method of tenacity. A way of fixing belief involving a steadfast adherence to a particular belief , regardless of contrary arguments; see empirical (p. 32). Believing the President is working in the best interest of the nation despite evidence to the contrary, because it is stressful to think the government is corrupt.

Organization. One function of a theory is to collect or organize what is known into a coherent statement (p. 41). The theory of diffusion of responsibility organizes a large amount of data about social loafing.

Parsimony. A good, powerful theory should explain many events with few statements or explanatory concepts; thus refers to simplicity (p. 46). One theory such as addiction can explain drug taking behavior in rats and humans rather than trying to use different theories for each situation.

Precision. A good theory should be precise in its predictions (p. 46). A theory in the form of a mathematical equation is better than one that uses loose verbal statements.

Prediction. A specification of relationships resulting from correlational methods; also one aim of a theory (p. 41). Assuming the outcome of an experiment based on a theory.

Scientific method. According to Pierce, this method fixes belief on the basis of experience; see empirical (p.33). Using evidence from observations to determine how long it takes for our eyes to adapt to darkness rather than believing how long it takes based on an authority such as a professor.

Self-correcting. Science is self-correcting because it relies on public, empirical observations; old beliefs are discarded if they do not fit the empirical data (p. 33). Abandoning the idea that the hormone estrogen is only important for female sexual behavior when it was demonstrated that estrogen also affects memory and learning.

Social loafing. The decrease in individual effort that sometimes occurs when other people are present and when group performance is measured (p. 30). If you have five friends helping you move, they will be less likely to work hard than if you had one friend helping.

Strong inference. Platt's view that scientific progress comes about through a series of tests of alternative theoretical outcomes (p. 38). Designing experiments that will rule out alternate theories to explain a phenomenon.

Testability. A good theory of ideas whose purpose is to describe and predict. (p. 46). The theory that life started with Adam and Eve cannot be directly tested and therefore falsified ; therefore it is a poor theory.

Theory. A collection of ideas whose purpose is to describe and predict (p. 43). Einstein's theory of Relativity predicts the nature of planetary movement.

Workload. The amount of attention-demanding effort imposed on a person (p. 42). When air traffic controllers work too many hours, i.e. high workload, there is risk of air mishaps.

KEY TERM MATCHING

1.	
___ a priori method ___ method of authority ___ method of tenacity ___ scientific method ___ what each of the above is	a. a way to fix belief b. characteristic of bigots c. empirical and self-correcting d. the Bible told me so e. the sun will rise in the east tomorrow
2.	

___ applied research
 	
 ___ basic research
 	
 ___ data
 	
 ___ deduction
 	
 ___ falsifiability view
 	
 ___ induction
 	
 ___ strong inference
 	
 ___ theory
	a. aimed at solving a real-world problem
	 b. aimed at understanding the processes
	     underlying behavior
	 c. derivation of theory from data
	 d. empirical observations
	 e. organizes existing data and predicts new data
	 f. pitting possible outcomes against each other to
	     decide between competing theories
	 g. prediction of data from theory
	 h. useful theories must be capable of being
	     disproved

3.	
___ parsimony ___ precision ___ testability ___ what each of the above is	a. can be shown to be false b. criterion for evaluating a theory c. the fewer the statements, the better d. the more exact the prediction, the better

4.	a. an intervening variable
___ diffusion of responsibility	b. people work less hard in a group than when alone
___ social loafing	c. a possible reason for b.
___ workload	

FILL IN THE BLANK

1. The phenomenon of people working less hard in groups than alone is called _____
_____ .

2. Social loafing may be a special case of a more general social phenomenon called _____ of _____ .

3. According to the American philosopher Charles Sanders Pierce, the simplest way of fixing belief is the method of _____ .

4. The method of fixing beliefs in which one refuses to alter their acquired knowledge regardless of evidence to the contrary is known as the method of _____ .

5. In the scientific method of fixing beliefs, beliefs are fixed on the basis of _____ .

6. Scientific psychology is characterized as being _____ and _____ -correcting.

7. In the inductive approach to science, reasoning proceeds from particular _____ to a general _____ . The opposite occurs in the _____ approach to science.

8. The _____ scientist believes that general explanatory principles will emerge once enough data have been collected.

9. According to the _____ approach to theories, data are useful only in the evaluation of a theoretical explanation.

10. According to Popper, the philosopher of science, good theories must be _____ .

11. Experiments designed to pit two hypotheses against each other in the hope of eliminating one of them involve the process of _____ _____ .

12. One function of a theory is to provide a framework for _____ existing data.

13. Theories may be used to generate _____ for situations where no data have yet been obtained. The two functions of a theory known as organization and prediction are sometimes called _____ and _____ , respectively.

14. An abstract concept that relates independent and dependent variables is called an
_____ _____ .

15. Intervening variables, by reducing the number of links necessary to relate independent and dependent variables, provide _____ in explanation.

16. A good theory will make very _____ predictions.

17. In evaluating theories, the criterion of _____ holds that the fewer the concepts a theory needs in order to explain various phenomena, the better the theory.

18. Theories having mathematical formulations are said to have greater _____ than those using only verbal statements.

19. A theory that cannot be _____ can never be disproved.
20. What distinguishes one science from another is the different _____ that are used.
21. Psychologists try to understand the underlying _____ that lead to behavior rather than the physical situations that produce behaviors.

MULTIPLE CHOICE
1. The tendency of people to work less hard in groups is known as
   a. diffusion of effort.
   b. social irresponsibility.
   c. social loafing.
   d. good sense.

2. Experiments have shown that people work just as hard in a group as when they work alone if
   a. good performance is rewarded.
   b. "team spirit" is high.
   c. the group leader is autocratic.
   d. each individual's performance is monitored.

3. The simplest way of fixing beliefs is
   a. the a priori method.
   b. the method of authority.
   c. the method of tenacity.
   d. the scientific method.

4. After listening to a lecture by an astronaut who conducted experiments aboard the space shuttle, you now believe that plants can germinate in space. This belief was fixed by
   a. the method of authority.
   b. the method of tenacity.
   c. the scientific method.
   d. the empirical method.

5. Your roommate asks whether you believe that sunbathing can increase one's chances of getting skin cancer. You reply that of course it can because "baking in the sun is bound to be harmful to skin tissue." This belief was probably fixed by
   a. the a priori method.
   b. the method of authority.
   c. the scientific method.
   d. the method of tenacity.

6. Fixing belief a priori refers to
   a. appealing to higher authorities.
   b. believing views that seem reasonable.
   c. believing opinions based on systematic observation.
   d. believing only facts and not unsupported opinions.

7. A disadvantage of fixing beliefs by the method of authority or a priori is that
   a. neither method involves systematic observation.
   b. neither method offers a way of deciding which of two beliefs is superior to the other.
   c. neither method results in beliefs that are precise or testable.
   d. both a and b

8. The scientific method is the preferred technique for satisfying curiosity because it
   a. relies on systematic observation.
   b. is self-correcting.
   c. provides an empirical basis for fixing belief.
   d. all of the above

9. The _____ scientist emphasizes data and the _____ scientist emphasizes theory.
   a. inductive; deductive
   b. empirical; inductive
   c. deductive; inductive
   d. deductive; empirical

10. The inductive scientist
    a. conducts research in order to gain support for a particular theoretical view.
    b. believes that organized patterns of important empirical relations will emerge once enough data are collected.
    c. is not concerned with empirical observation.
    d. none of the above

11. The deductive scientist
    a. conducts research in order to gain support for a particular theoretical view.
    b. believes that organizational patterns will emerge once enough data are collected.
    c. is concerned primarily with empirical observation.
    d. none of the above

12. Which of the following is true concerning inductive and deductive scientists?
   a.   Inductive scientists are more important because they provide basic data upon which to build theories.
   b.   Deductive scientists are more important because they try to bring order out of the mass of data collected by empiricists.
   c.   Most psychologists take either a purely inductive or purely deductive approach.
   d.   none of the above

13. According to the falsifiability view of theories proposed by Popper, _____ in evaluating a theory.
   a.   negative evidence is more important than positive evidence
   b.   positive evidence is more important than negative evidence
   c.   replications of theories is most important
   d.   proving the unreliability of a theory is most important

14. One key aspect of the falsifiability view of theories is that falsifiability depends upon _____.
   a.   fabricating data
   b.   unreliable data
   c.   empirical observations
   d.   theoretical deductions

15. Which of the following procedures should, in the ideal case, yield one theory if the process is used repeatedly?
   a.   deductive reasoning
   b.   inductive reasoning
   c.   hypothesis testing
   d.   strong inference

16. Theories
   a.   serve to organize existing data.
   b.   generate predictions for situations where no data have yet been collected.
   c.   can never be proven to be true.
   d.   all of the above

17. Intervening variables serve to connect
   a.   data and theory.
   b.   hypothesis and experiment.
   c.   independent and dependent variables.
   d.   deduction and induction.

18. Inclusion of intervening variables may make a theory more
    a.   precise.
    b.   testable.
    c.   parsimonious.
    d.   valid.

19. Theories with mathematical formulations are said to be more _____ than verbal theories.
    a.   parsimonious
    b.   correct
    c.   precise
    d.   provable

20. If a theory is not _____, it can never be disproved.
    a.   parsimonious
    b.   precise
    c.   testable
    d.   mathematical

21. Which of the following is true?
    a.   Data that are partially consistent with a theory can cause the theory to be modified.
    b.   Data that are inconsistent with a theory can lead to the rejection of that theory.
    c.   Data that are consistent with a theory can never prove the theory.
    d.   All of the above.

22. A scientist theorizes that if all males were removed from society, the incidence of violent crime would decrease by at least 80%. The major problem with this hypotheses is that it is not _____.
    a.   precise
    b.   testable
    c.   parsimonious
    d.   reliable

23. If a theory cannot be potentially disproved,
    a.   it is said to be unparsimonious.
    b.   it is said to be testable.
    c.   it is useless to scientists.
    d.   none of the above

24. The fact that the relationship between basic psychological research and pressing social issues is not immediately obvious
    a. suggests that psychology has little to offer in the way of improving society.
    b. does not mean that no such relationship actually exists.
    c. means that federal funding should be withheld from psychological research.
    d. suggests that psychologists are studying the wrong problems.

25. Psychologists
    a. are more interested in physical situations that produce behavior rather than in the underlying process.
    b. are interested in neither physical situations nor underlying processes that produce behavior.
    c. are more interested in underlying processes that produce behavior than in physical situations.
    d. none of the above

TRUE FALSE
1. The method of authority involves taking someone else's word on faith.
2. Religious beliefs are generally formed by the method of tenacity.
3. An advantage of the scientific method over other methods of fixing beliefs is that it offers a means of determining the "superiority" of one belief over another.
4. Scientific data are necessarily empirical observations.
5. All approaches to science involve data and theory.
6. According to the inductive approach to science, general explanations are arrived at from a set of theoretical statements that can then be tested against data.
7. Theories induced from empirical observations are tentative due to the limited scope of the available data.
8. Deductive approaches to science emphasize the primacy, or primary role, of theory.
9. Many correct predictions made by a theory can help to prove the theory to be correct.
10. A theory may never be proved.
11. The purposes of a psychological theory are to describe and explain behavior.
12. Intervening variables serve to link observables to non-observables.
13. Inclusion of intervening variables makes theories less parsimonious than they would otherwise be.
14. If two theories can account for the same data, but Theory A uses 10 statements and Theory B uses 15, then Theory B is the better theory.
15. One function of a scientific theory is to allow scientists to generate predictions for situations where no data have yet been obtained.
16. The criterion of parsimony is most concerned with the number of findings a theory can account for.
17. A theory may be precise without being testable.
18. Applied research inevitably precedes basic research.

19. According to the text, the inability to predict which basic research being done today will have an impact on society years from now means that we should stop doing basic research.
20. Basic researchers generally assume that different mental processes occur across different physical situations.
21. Establishing similar physical situations in which to observe behavior guarantees similarity in the mental processes underlying the behaviors.

EXPERIMENTAL DILEMMAS

(I)   Two researchers are studying the effects of marijuana on personal motivation. Both experimenters believe that chronic marijuana use is associated with a decline in motivation level, but they have different ways of studying the problem. Researcher A hypothesizes that "Grade point average decreases logarithmically with the number of marijuana cigarettes smoked per week." Researcher B's hypothesis states that "People who smoke marijuana have less drive to succeed than people who do not smoke marijuana." Which experimenter has a better research hypothesis? Why?

(II)   From the application box in the main text (p. 35) the authors refer to a study by Wason where subjects were more likely to select numerical sequences that would confirm their own hypothesis rather than those that would falsify it.

> 1)   From the example given in the application box, write three possible hypotheses to explain the rule governing the series 2, 4, 6
> 2)   Pick one of your hypotheses and write one possible series, which could confirm if it is true while ruling out others.

ANSWER KEY
Key Term Matching
1. e, d, b, c, a
2. a, b, d, g, h, c, f, e
3. c, d, a, b
4. c, b, a

Fill in the Blank
1.   social loafing (p. 30)
2.   diffusion of responsibility (p. 31)
3.   authority (p. 32)
4.   tenacity (p. 32)
5.   observation (p. 33)
6.   empirical, self (p. 33)
7.   observation, theory, deductive (p.34-35)

8. inductive (p. 35)
9. deductive (p. 35)
10. falsifiable (p. 37)
11. strong inference (p. 38)
12. organizing (p. 41)
13. predictions (p. 41), description, explanation (p. 42)
14. intervening variable (p. 43)
15. economy (p. 46)
16. precise (p. 46)
17. parsimony (p.46)
18. precision (p. 46)
19. tested (p. 46)
20. techniques (p. 51-52)
21. processes (p. 51-52)

Multiple Choice

1. c (p. 30)	10. b (p. 35)	18. b (p. 43)
2. d (p. 30)	11. a (p. 35)	19. c (p. 46)
3. a (p. 32)	12. d (pp. 35-37)	20. c (p. 46)
4. a (p. 32)	13. a (p. 37)	21. d (p. 47)
5. a (p. 33)	14. d (p. 37)	22. b (p. 46)
6. b (p. 33)	15. d (p. 38)	23. d (pp. 46-47)
7. d (p. 33)	16. c (p. 41)	24. b (pp. 50-52)
8. d (p. 33)	17. c (p. 43)	25. c (p. 51)
9. a (p. 35)		

True False

1. T (p. 32)	12. F (p.43)
2. F (p. 32)	13. F (p. 43)
3. T (p. 33)	14. F (p. 46)
4. T (p. 33)	15. T (p. 41)
5. T (p. 33)	16. F (p. 46)
6. F (p. 35)	17. T (p. 46)
7. T (p. 35-36)	18. F (p. 50)
8. T (p. 35-36)	19. F (p. 50)
9. F (p. 37)	20. F (p. 50)
10. T (p. 37)	21. F (p. 51)
11. T (p. 41)	

Experimental Dilemmas

(I)

Researcher A has a better hypothesis because it is specific and testable.

(II)

1) There could be any number of hypotheses, here are a few examples....

Numbers are even and in increasing order

Numbers increase by 2

Numbers are below 10

Numbers can be divided into 24 by a whole number

2) For the first hypothesis, you could select 12, 20, and 22. This would confirm that hypothesis and rule out the others. Can you think of others?

FURTHER READINGS
To learn more about the idea of **social loafing** and its research implications see:

Karau, S.J. & Williams, K.D. (2001). Understanding individual motivation in groups: The collective effort model. In M.E. Turner (Ed.), *Groups at work: Theory and research. Applied social research* (pp. 113-141). Mahwah, NJ: Lawrence Erlbaum Associates.

Boersema (2003) provides a summary of Pierce's account of scientific explanation.

Boersema, D. (2003). Pierce on explanation. *Journal of Speculative Philosophy, 17,* 224-236.

WEB RESOURCES
For an interesting perspective on the origins of **scientific psychology**, you can read a seminar by W.R. Street from Central Washington University at:
http://www.cwu.edu/~warren/shipwrecks.htm

You can also find information about scientific explanation at the Stanford Encyclopedia of Philosophy (http://plato.stanford.edu/entries/scientific-explanation/).

Chapter 3

Exploring the Literature of Psychology

SUMMARY
1. How to do a Literature Search
    1.1. Literature Searches
        1.1.1.   are useful to find out
            1.1.1.1. if others have already done your proposed experiment
            1.1.1.2. "tricks of the trade" that may be useful in designing an experiment
        1.1.2.   Useful general resources include
            1.1.2.1. **Psychological Abstracts** which contains brief abstract of articles from most journals that publish psychological research
            1.1.2.2. **Computerized literature searches** are very efficient in generating a list of appropriate articles
            1.1.2.3. **Social Science Citation Index** lists recent articles that reference a critical article
2. Parts of an Article
    2.1. **Title** and **Author**(s)
        2.1.1.   titles often state the independent and dependent variables
        2.1.2.   familiar authors often identify articles of interest
    2.2. **Abstract** - a concise summary of the article
    2.3. **Introduction**
        2.3.1.   Specifies problem to be studied
        2.3.2.   Reviews relevant literature
        2.3.3.   Specifies the research hypothesis
    2.4. **Method**
        2.4.1.   Contains enough information to allow replication of the study
        2.4.2.   Usually divided into subsections:
            2.4.2.1. **Participants** - how many, how selected, who they were, special characteristics
            2.4.2.2. **Apparatus** or **Materials** - equipment or questionnaires, etc. used to test the subjects
            2.4.2.3. **Procedure** - explains what happened to the subjects
    2.5. **Results**
        2.5.1.   Summarized data
        2.5.2.   Descriptive statistics
        2.5.3.   **Tables**
        2.5.4.   **Figures** are graphs that plot the
            2.5.4.1. dependent variable on the Y axis or **ordinate**
            2.5.4.2. independent variable on the X axis or **abscissa**

  2.5.5. Inferential statistics are used to determine how sure we can be that any differences between treatment conditions are not due to chance
  2.6. **Discussion** - an interpretation of the results
  2.7. **References** - bibliographic citations for articles referenced in the current study
3. Checklist for the Critical Reader
  3.1. after reading the introduction, you should know
   3.1.1. the author's goal
   3.1.2. what hypothesis is tested
   3.1.3. how *you* would test this hypothesis
  3.2. after reading the **method,** you should
   3.2.1. consider whether your proposed method is better than the author's
   3.2.2. consider whether the author's method actually tests the hypothesis
   3.2.3. identify the dependent, independent, and control variables
   3.2.4. predict what you think will happen in the experiment
  3.3. after reading the **results,** you should decide
   3.3.1. whether the results were unexpected
   3.3.2. how you would interpret the obtained results
   3.3.3. what applications and implications would you draw from your interpretation
  3.4. After reading the **discussion,** you should decide
   3.4.1. whether your interpretation or the author's best represents the data
   3.4.2. whether you or the author offers the most cogent discussion of the applications and implications of the results

LEARNING THE TERMINOLOGY

Abscissa. The horizontal axis (or X-axis) in a graph (p. 63)

Abstract. Short summary at the beginning of a journal article that informs the reader about the results (p. 60)

Apparatus. A subsection of the method portion of a technical paper that describes any special equipment used in the research to test participants (p. 61)

Author. The person or persons responsible for a technical paper; a literature search via an author's name (p. 60)

Computerized literature search. A method of searching the database in a library that uses a computer (p. 59)

Discussion A section of a technical paper in which the author draws theoretical conclusions by examining, interpreting, and qualifying the results (p. 67)

Figures. Graphical presentations of data in the results sections of a research report (p. 63)

Introduction. The portion of a technical paper that specifies the problem to be studied and tells why it is important (p. 61)

Materials. A part of the method section in which elements other than the apparatus used to test participants are described, including surveys, videos, words presented for memorization, and the like (p. 61)

Method. A section of a technical paper that describes in detail the operations performed by the experimenter (p. 61)

Mozart effect. The finding of better performance on spatial-temporal tasks following exposure to music composed by Mozart; the exact mechanisms underlying the effect (including whether it may be due to an experimental artifact) are still under debate (p. 71)

Ordinate. The vertical axis (or y-axis) in a graph (p. 63)

Participants/subjects. A subsection of the method section indicating the number and manner of selecting the participants (humans) or subjects (nonhuman animals) in the research (p. 61)

Procedure. A subsection of the method section of a technical paper that explains what happened to the participants/subjects and contains enough information that someone else could repeat the study exactly as it was done (p. 61)

Psychological Abstracts. A journal produced by the APA that lists abstracts of most of the journal articles relevant to psychological topics (p. 57)

PsycINFO. A computerized database containing abstracts of most psychological journals (p. 59)

References. Found at the end of a technical paper; only articles cited in the text are included it the reference section (p. 67)

Results. A section of a technical paper that tells what happened in the research (p. 61)

Social Science Citation Index. A journal containing lists of articles that cite a particular author or work (p. 59)

Tables. A non-graphical way of summarizing data in a technical paper. Summary values of the dependent variable are presented under headings describing the levels of the independent variable (p. 62)

Title. Provides an idea of the contents of an article or technical paper and usually states only the dependent and independent variables (p. 60)

KEY TERM MATCHING

1.	
____ abscissa ____ figure ____ ordinate ____ PsychINFO ____ *Psychological Abstracts* ____ references ____ *Social Science Citation Index* ____ tables	a. citations of articles referred to in present article b. computerized psychological data base c. collection of summaries of research articles d. graph of summarized data e. lists recent articles that reference a target article f. non-graphical data summary g. where dependent variable is plotted h. where independent variable is plotted
2.	
____ apparatus ____ author ____ abstract ____ discussion ____ introduction ____ materials ____ method ____ participants ____ procedure ____ results ____ title	a. appears after the title on the first page b. describes equipment used in study c. where inferential statistics are used d. names independent and dependent variables e. presents enough information for study to be replicated f. summary of the key points of article g. what happens to the participant h. where a questionnaire would be presented i. where problem is presented j. where results are interpreted k. where selection of participants is described

FILL-IN-THE-BLANK

1. The seven parts of a basic psychology article are a)_____ and _____, b)_____, c)_____, d)_____, e)_____, f)_____, and g)_____.
2. Most titles state the _____ and _____ variables.
3. The _____ is a short paragraph that summarizes the key points of the article.
4. The references are found at the _____ of an article.
5. Any published reports cited in a paper are listed in the _____. The Introduction should specify the _____ to be studied, the _____ to be tested and the rationale behind any _____.
6. If you wanted to replicate an experiment you would need to consult the _____ section in the article that describes the experiment.

7. The Method section is sometimes divided up into three subsections that cover: _____, _____, and _____.
8. The _____ section contains a summary of what happened in the experiment.
9. The Method section should contain _____ _____ to allow _____ of the study.
10. In the Results section, _____ statistics used to summarize the data and _____ statistics are used to examine differences between groups or conditions.
11. If different figures are included in an article it is important to check that the _____ are comparable so that effects can be compared across figures.
12. Extra skepticism (on the part of the reader) is required when reading the _____ section.
13. Before you read the Method section you should try to design a(n) _____ to test the _____ stated in the Introduction.
14. After you have read the Method section you should check to see that the methods used are adequate for testing the _____.
15. You should try to predict the results for the experiment before reading the _____ section.

MULTIPLE CHOICE
1. In which of the following sources would you not generally expect to find review articles?
   a. American Psychologist
   b. Journal of Experimental Social Psychology
   c. Psychological Bulletin
   d. Psychological Review

2. Perhaps the best place to start in developing a list of references for a problem in psychology that is new to you is
   a. American Journal of Psychology.
   b. The American Psychologist.
   c. Annual Review of Psychology.
   d. Psychological Abstracts.
   e. Social Science Citation Index.

3. A journal that allows you to identify recent articles that have referenced a critical key article is
   a. Current Contents.
   b. Annual Review of Psychology.
   c. Bulletin of the Psychonomic Society.
   d. Social Science Citation Index.

4. Each of the following is a part of a journal article except the _____.
   a. introduction
   b. method
   c. results
   d. discussion
   e. summary

5. Which of the following is least likely to appear in the title?
   a. a special subject characteristic
   b. independent variable
   c. dependent variable
   d. research implications

6. A well-written abstract should _____.
   a. rely on information in the paper to be fully understood
   b. refer to information not in the paper
   c. be self-contained
   d. have a lot of abbreviations to reduce length

7. In the "Introduction" of a journal article the author should
   a. specify the problem to be studied.
   b. specify the hypothesis (or hypotheses) to be tested.
   c. give the rationale behind any predictions.
   d. all of the above

8. Which of the following should be included in the "Method" section of a journal article?
   a. considerations concerning subjects
   b. a description of the apparatus used in the experiment
   c. the procedure of the experiment
   d. all of the above
   e. both a and b

9. If you conducted a study in which you administered a questionnaire, which of the following details about the questionnaire is NOT an unimportant detail for replication?
   a. font and appearance of items
   b. number of items
   c. paper orientation
   d. type of pencil needed

10. Which of the following would be unusual to find in the "Results" section of a journal article?
   a. raw data
   b. summary statistics
   c. inferential statistics
   d. the level of significance

11. The interpretation of the experimental findings is found in the _____.
    a. abstract
    b. introduction
    c. method
    d. results
    e. discussion

12. The question "What hypothesis will be tested?" should be answered by reading the _____.
    a. abstract
    b. introduction
    c. method
    d. results
    e. discussion

13. The question "What is the independent variable?" should be answered by reading the

    _____.
    a. abstract
    b. introduction
    c. method
    d. results
    e. discussion

14. The question "Are the results expected?" should be answered by reading the _____.
    a. abstract
    b. introduction
    c. method
    d. results
    e. discussion

15. The question "Is my interpretation better than the author's?" should be answered by reading
    the _____.
    a. abstract
    b. introduction
    c. method
    d. results
    e. discussion

TRUE-FALSE
1. The introduction of a journal article specifies the hypothesis to be studied and briefly describes the experiment designed to test the hypothesis.
2. Statistical design features of an experiment are described in the "Method" section of a journal article.
3. The statement "$F(6,20) = 7.40$, p $= .01$" means that the odds for obtaining an F-statistic at least as large as 7.40 by chance if the experiment were repeated would be one percent.

4. In the "Discussion" section of a journal article, the author is free to interpret the results, and thus the reader must accept the author's interpretation.
5. The most important question for the reader to answer after reading the "Method" section is: Is this how I would design an experiment to test this hypothesis?

EXPERIMENTAL DILEMMA

You are asked to develop a research proposal for the Research Methods class. You are required to cite at least relevant 10 journal articles in your proposal. After thinking about the areas in psychology you find interesting and carefully observing fellow students on your dorm floor, you decide to examine the relationship between introversion and computer games. You logon to *PsycInfo* and search on "introversion" and find 1301 articles. You then search on "computer games" and find another 662 articles. Unfortunately, after combining the searches you find only two references and they are both dissertations from 1987. Disappointed, and somewhat surprised that you did not find articles dealing with your idea, you start considering other options. What should you do?

EXPERIMENTAL PROJECT

The best way to get good at reading journal articles is through practice. The more articles you read the more proficient you will become at reading reports. Each time you read an article you should try to answer all of the suggested questions for critical readers). For further practice reading journal articles, consult your university library. Research articles in the *Psychonomic Bulletin & Review* are good for practice reading, since there is a page limit for the articles that appear in that journal. Finally, it is a good idea to get together with classmates and decide upon one or more articles to read. After you have read the articles(s) and written out your answers to the questions, you should compare you answers with your classmates.

ANSWERS
Key Term Matching
1. h, d, g, b, c, a, e, f
2. b, a, f, j, I, h, e, k, g, c, d

Fill-in-the-blank
1. title, author(s), b) abstract, c) introduction, d) method, e) results, f) discussions, g) references (p. 60)
2. dependent, independent (p. 60)
3. abstract (p. 60)
4. end (p. 67)
5. references, problem, hypothesis, predictions (p. 61)
6. method (p. 61)
7. participants, apparatus or materials, procedure (p. 61)
8. results (p. 61)
9. enough information, replication (p. 61)
10. descriptive, inferential (p. 61)
11. scales (p. 65)

12. discussion (p. 67)
13. method, hypothesis (p. 68)
14. hypothesis (p. 68)
15. results (p. 68)

Multiple Choice

1. b (pp. 57-58)
2. d (p. 57)
3. d (p. 59)
4. e (pp. 61, 67)
5. d (p. 60)
6. c (pp. 60-61)
7. d (p. 61)
8. d (p. 61)

9. b (p. 61)
10. a (p. 61)
11. e (p. 67)
12. b (p. 68)
13. c (p. 68)
14. d (p. 69)
15. e (p. 70)

True or False

1. F (p. 61)
2. T (p. 61)
3. F (p. 66)

4. T (p. 67)
5. F (p. 68)

Research Dilemma

You should not abandon your idea. The key to finding relevant information in any database is knowing what terms to use and when to restrict or expand your search. In this case, "introversion" is a "personality trait". If you expand your search term from "introversion" to "personality" in *PsycInfo* you will find 145,864 articles. When you combine "personality" and "computer games" you will find 75 articles. These articles will give you enough articles to build a case for examining introversion and computer gaming.

FURTHER READINGS

American Psychological Association (1992). *PsycINFO user manual*. Washington, DC: American Psychological Association.
This text is APA's extensive guide to conducting a literature search using either *PsycLIT* or *PsycINFO*. Covered topics include the formation of basic search strategies, command structures, use of keywords, and tips for more advanced users, as well as the history and extent of the databases.

WEB RESOURCES

The American Psychological Association Science Directorate provides an online version of a pamphlet that is designed to help novices conduct a literature search. The pamphlet introduces students to both *PsycINFO* and *Psychological Abstracts*, and also mentions *The Thesaurus of Psychological Index Terms* as a helpful guide to finding appropriate keywords. A list of additional APA resources also is provided, including free search guides and journal information on *PsycINFO*. http://www.apa.org/science/lib.html

PSYCLINE (owned by Armin Günther) is an extensive, online, searchable database of journals in psychology and the social sciences. The database can be searched using key words, major subdiscipline, limited content (e.g., abstracts), or alphabetically. A limited summary is provided about the focus of each journal. Links also are provided to the journal websites, where more detailed information about journal contents, sample articles, editorial staff, and subscription should be found. http://www.psycline.org/journals/psycline.html

RESEARCH METHODS WORKSHOPS
The *Evaluating Published Research* tutorial at the *Wadsworth Research Methods Workshops* site allows you to evaluate a sample article. There are questions at the end of each section of the paper regarding paper content and form. The *Wadsworth's Research Methods Workshops* can be found at: http://psychology.wadsworth.com/workshops/.

Chapter 4

Observations in Psychological Research

SUMMARY
1. Descriptive Observation Methods
    1.1. **descriptive observations** record the quantity and frequency of behaviors
    1.2. three types of observational methods
        1.2.1. **naturalistic observations**
        1.2.2. **case study**
        1.2.3. **survey**
    1.3. Naturalistic Observations
        1.3.1. **ethology** – study of naturally occurring behaviors
            1.3.1.1. **ethogram** is a relatively complete list of behaviors that a researcher uses to record behavior
            1.3.1.2. **interobserver** reliability measures the degree to which two or more observers agree when looking at the same behavior
    1.4. The Case Study
        1.4.1. a case study is an intensive investigation of a case involving only a few people
            1.4.1.1. typically descriptive and do not allow for firm inferences (although can lead to reasonable guesses)
            1.4.1.2. **deviant-case analysis** compares two cases that are similar but have different outcomes
    1.5. Survey Research
        1.5.1. collect limited information from a relatively large sample
        1.5.2. leads to descriptive results
        1.5.3. want a representative sample
            1.5.3.1. **random sampling** is when each person in the population has the same probability of being surveyed
2. Advantages of Descriptive Observations
    2.1. useful in the beginning stages of research to get an idea about what factors are important and the range of behaviors of interest (i.e., helps define problems and raise questions)
    2.2. can serve an **ecological function** of examining naturally occurring behavior (high **ecological validity**)
    2.3. cannot determine how factors are related (i.e., do not allow for causal statements)
3. Sources of Error in Descriptive Research
    3.1. difficult to asses relations among events

3.2. often difficult to reproduce

3.3. researcher bias – make interpretive instead of descriptive observations (i.e., begin to make inferences based on preconceptions instead of being an objective observer)

4. Reactivity in Descriptive Research

    4.1. participants, based on cues within the study, perceive a *role* to fill within the research context and adjust their behavior accordingly (**subject (participant) role**)

    4.2. can minimize reactivity in naturalistic observation by using unobtrusive observations or unobtrusive measures

        4.2.1. **unobtrusive observations** – the person or animal is unaware of being observed

            4.2.1.1. **participant observation** – used when the participants or environment require close contact

        4.2.2. **unobtrusive measures** – indirect observations of behavior by looking at the result or product of behavior instead of the behavior itself

    4.3. **case studies** are retrospective in nature and therefore suffer from inaccuracies due to ordinary forgetting and **motivated forgetting**

    4.4. surveys, interviews, and tests can be inaccurate due to **response style** or *response sets*

        4.4.1. **response acquiescence**

        4.4.2. **response deviation**

        4.4.3. **social desirability**

        4.4.4. **forced-choice tests** that force participants to choice between equally desirable is one method for eliminating response bias

        4.4.5. the **volunteer problem** highlights the difference between those who volunteer to participate in research and those that do not

LEARNING THE TERMINOLOGY

Case Study. Intensive investigation of a particular instance, or cases, of some behavior; does not allow inferences of cause and effect but is merely descriptive (pp. 89-90). Describing the treatment effects of a person with a very rare condition such as a fear of balloons because there are too few people with that condition to conduct a true study.

Demand Characteristics. Those cues available to participants in an experiment that may enable them to determine the purpose of the experiment, or what the experimenter expects (p. 102). An experimenter wishes to know how people feel about a new law on local oil drilling. If the questions were to include ideas that oil drilling was wrong or that it may hurt the environment, then the survey would be producing demand characteristics. Of course nobody wants others to think that they want to hurt baby seals!

Descriptive Observations. Observations of the type, quantity, and frequency of particular behaviors, and do not try to provide causal explanations of those behaviors (p. 89).

Deviant-Case Analysis. Investigation of similar cases that differ in outcome in an attempt to specify reasons for the different outcomes (p. 96). A psychologist has two patients with borderline personality disorder; one patient responds to behavior therapy while another does not. He conducts a deviant-case analysis to examine differences in these two patients and understand why one responded to therapy and the other did not.

Ecological Function. How behaviors help a person/animal adapt to its environment (p. 98). Memory function may seem very different in 3 and 4 year old infants the lab but in the real world it may not. This is because it depends upon the environment that these infants are in, both ages adapt very well to their respective environments.

Ecological Validity. The extent to which a research setting matches the environment of the problem under investigation; a threat to external validity of experiments (p. 99). Testing mathematical ability of people in a lab and under experimental conditions may not be a true measure of their math ability in the real world when they are not the subject of an experiment.

Ethogram. A data sheet providing categories for making naturalistic observations (p. 92). Inventory of various actions produced by an animal engaged in a broad category of behavior such as aggression. In this case, an ethogram would show different aggressive behaviors such as biting, growling etc....

Ethology. The systematic study of behavior; usually animal behavior in natural settings (p. 92). Examining social interactions of gorillas in the wild.

Forced-Choice Test. Tests in which the participant must select between two or more statements; often used to control response styles (p. 105). A question in which the subjects must select between two alternatives of equal social desirability.

Interobserver Reliability. The degree to which two or more observers can accurately categorize naturalistic observations (p. 93). Two students share the responsibility for observing maternal care in rats. How their observations do not differ is a measure of interobserver reliability.

Motivated Forgetting. Distortions of past events reported retrospectively because of the emotional nature of those events (p. 104). The idea that people reconstruct their past memories to match their current beliefs, such that a person would say they did more to help anti-terrorist activities a couple of years ago when really they did not.

Naturalistic Observations. Description of naturally occurring events without intervention on the part of the investigator (p. 89). Observing bear feeding behavior in the wild without giving the bear food or interfering with its search for food.

Participant Observation. An observation procedure in which the observer participates with those being observed (p. 103). Observing Gorilla behavior in the wild while living with them and being a part of their social community.

Random Sample. The obtained participants in a study such that each member of a population has an equal likelihood of being selected for participation (p. 97).

Reactivity. Term to describe observations that are influenced by (or may be a reaction to) the detected presence of the investigator (p. 102). Your dog eats its food faster because you are standing over it watching.

Response Acquiescence. A habitual way of responding on tests that involves frequently responding 'yes' (p. 105). It is in the nature of some people to mostly answer yes to questions.

Response Deviation. A habitual way of responding on tests that involves frequently responding 'no' (p. 105). Some people just like to say 'no' no matter what the question asks.

Response Style. A habitual way of answering questions on a questionnaire or survey (p. 105). Some people will mostly say 'yes' to questions, while others, perhaps in a bad mood, will answer 'no' to most questions on a survey. Two examples of response styles are *response acquiescence* and *response deviation*.

Retrospective Data. Data that were collected in the past. Often used in case studies (see p. 104). Looking back at old hospital records to determine whether stroke patients had highly stressful jobs.

Social Desirability. The tendency of subjects in survey research to give a socially acceptable (desirable) response (p. 105). In an experiment on drinking and driving, a subject may respond that it is wrong to drink and drive and state that they would never do this although they may do it habitually.

Subject Roles. The social and psychological factors present in a research situation that may influence the results (p. 102). When a subject tries to determine the purpose of the experiment and reacts accordingly (good-subject role). Other subject roles include negative-subject role, apprehensive-subject role, and faithful-subject role (refer to textbook).

Survey Research. The technique of obtaining a limited amount of information from a large number of people, usually through random sampling (p. 91). Asking questions on a particular topic (often in the form of a questionnaire) from many people that are usually representative of the larger population.

Unobtrusive Measures. Measures taken from the results of behavior, not the behavior itself. That is, when the behavior is observed *indirectly* by examining the results of behavior that has already occurred (p. 103). *E.g* one student videotapes a behavior while another scores that behavior from the tape.

Unobtrusive Observations. Observations not resulting in reactivity. That is, research in which the subjects are *unaware* that they are being observed (pp. 102-103). *Observing Gorillas in the wild that are unaware that the experimenter is there.*

Volunteer Problem. Volunteer subjects differ from those less eager to participate; may be a source of bias in research (p. 105). A study on the effects of alcohol on fearlessness may be biased by the fact that those subjects signing up for the study already drink alcohol whereas non-drinkers would be less likely to volunteer.

KEY TERM MATCHING

1.	
___descriptive observation ___meta-analysis ___naturalistic observation ___participant observation ___relational observation ___unobtrusive observation	a. observing how two or more behaviors go together b. determines the external validity of a treatment by examining many studies c. includes naturalistic observation, case studies and surveys d. most apt to be done by an ethologist e. non-reactive direct observation of behavior f. one way to study mountain gorillas
2.	
___response acquiescence ___response styles ___response deviation ___social desirability ___subject roles	a. response habits in answering questions b. social and psychological factors that might influence research results c. tendency to give a "no" answer d. tendency to give a "yes" answer e. tendency to give a socially acceptable answer
3.	
___anthropomorphizing ___case study	a. a small amount of data is gathered from a large sample b. attributing human characteristics to animals

___demand characteristics	c. derived from participant's memory
	d. intensive investigation of a single
___ethology	individual case of interest
	e. older term for subject reactivity
___reactivity	f. people willing to participate in research are
	different from those unwilling to
___retrospective	participate
	g. study of behavior in the natural
___survey	environment
	h. the act of observing behavior affects the
___volunteer problem	behavior

FILL IN THE BLANK

1. Examples of descriptive observations include _____ _____, the _____ _____ and _____.
2. Descriptive observations are a useful first step in research since they provide and extend the _____ that can lead to more controlled experimentation.
3. Descriptive observations alone cannot tell us how events are _____ to each other.
4. Descriptive observation, in particular the case study, is limited because the observations often cannot be _____.
5. _____ is the study of naturally occurring behavior (often in the wild).
6. A(n) _____ is an inventory of specific actions that a particular species might produce in one behavioral category.
7. _____ _____ refers to the agreement between two independent observers of the same behavior.
8. A(n)_____ _____ is an intensive investigation of a single case of some sort.
9. The _____-_____ _____ compares two individuals who are similar in many characteristics, but have different outcomes.
10. In _____ research, a small amount of data is collected from a large sample of people.
11. It is difficult to maintain a descriptive rather than interpretative level of observation, for example, avoiding _____, the attribution of human characteristics to animals.
12. When the process of observing behavior changes that behavior, the process is said to be _____.
13. Two general ways to guard against participant's reactions from ruining our research is to make unobtrusive _____ or make unobtrusive _____.
14. Unobtrusive measures are _____ observations of behavior.
15. _____ _____ is a way of making unobtrusive observations by gaining acceptance of the observed subjects.
16. Much of the evidence in a case study is _____ in nature.

17. A problem inherent in case studies is _____ _____: People often distort the memory of unpleasant events.
18. Tests and survey results may be contaminated by response _____ or _____ sets.
19. The forced-choice technique requires subjects to select between two alternatives of equal _____ _____.
20. One problem inherent in interpreting data from opinion surveys that rely on volunteer mailings is the _____ _____.

MULTIPLE CHOICE

1. The advantage of descriptive observation is that
   a. it allows for a good deal of experimental control.
   b. it allows for easy replication.
   c. it helps to define a problem area and raise interesting questions.
   d. it is primarily concerned with relationships.

2. A relatively complete inventory of specific behaviors performed by one species of animal, and that is useful in naturalistic observation is a(n)
   a. ethogram.
   b. response catalog.
   c. survey.
   d. protocol.

3. An intensive investigation of a particular person, or a particular group of people is called
   a. a case study.
   b. an ethogram.
   c. relational research.
   d. a survey.

4. In a deviant-case analysis, the researcher
   a. conducts an intensive investigation of an unusual individual.
   b. conducts naturalistic observations in an environment populated by deviants.
   c. investigates the relationships of an unusual person.
   d. considers two cases with many similarities but that differ in the outcome.

5. Assume that you are conducting an observational study on the effect of caffeine intake on test performance. In this study, you decide to collect responses to questionnaires from a group of college students who vary in study behavior and daily intake of caffeine. This is an example of _____.
   a. naturalistic observation
   b. a survey approach
   c. a case study
   d. a deviant-case analysis

6. When you brought a new puppy home, your old dog Spot bit you on the ankle. Calling Spot 'jealous' is an example of
   a. anthropomorphism.
   b. deviant-case study.
   c. naturalistic observation.
   d. concept validity.

7. The primary problem unique to descriptive observation is that it
   a. does not allow us to assess the relations among events.
   b. suffers from external invalidity.
   c. is only concerned with deviant cases.
   d. cannot be quantified.

8. Unobtrusive measures are
   a. direct observations taken without the awareness of the individual(s) being observed.
   b. indirect observations of behavior.
   c. obtained through participant observation.
   d. best avoided in naturalistic observations.

9. Which of the following does not pose a problem when attempting to interpret the results of a case study?
   a. the evidence is retrospective
   b. memory is fallible
   c. incomplete records
   d. anthropomorphizing

10. Which of the following is not a type of response style?
    a. response acquiescence
    b. response deviation
    c. social adaptability
    d. social desirability

11. A forced choice test procedure is an effort to
    a. avoid response-style problems.
    b. avoid motivated forgetting.
    c. solve the volunteer problem.
    d. remove demand characteristics.

12. Subject reactivity refers to the problem of
    a. subjects misinterpreting the experimenter's instructions.
    b. the influence of the expectations of the experimenter on the experimental results.
    c. the subjects' behavior being influenced by being in an experiment.
    d. treatment carryover effects.

13. Reactivity can be minimized in observational research by
    a. using a double-blind procedure.
    b. using unobtrusive measures.
    c. employing a placebo.
    d. participant observation.

14. Response style refers to
    a. demand characteristics in field research.
    b. reconstructive processes in retrospective memory.
    c. a habitual way of answering a question.
    d. knowing how your subjects will respond.

15. The "volunteer problem" refers to
    a. the problem associated with getting people to participate in psychological experiments.
    b. people who volunteer differ in many ways from people who do not volunteer.
    c. the ethics of using volunteers in experimentation.
    d. identifying a sample of people who are likely to volunteer for an experiment.

TRUE FALSE
1. Case studies can only include one subject.
2. Naturalistic observation is inherently unsystematic in the way that data is collected.
3. The text suggests that descriptive observation is not inferior to, but simply prior to experimentation.
4. Ethology refers to the study of naturally occurring behavior (often in the wild).
5. A lab experiment has more problems with ecological validity than naturalistic observation.
6. Descriptive observations are always reproducible.
7. Anthropomorphizing can only occur in naturalistic observation.
8. A large random sample is the surest way to obtain a representative sample for survey research.

EXPERIMENTAL DILEMMAS

(I)   A psychologist decides to examine how food availability affects female prairie vole sexual behaviors. He observes and records female vole sexual interactions in an area where there is a drought versus and area where there is plenty of food. He finds that in the non-drought area, the female prairie vole expresses a higher number of sexual behaviors in the presence of male prairie voles. He concludes that lack of nutrition decreases sexual behaviors in these female voles.

1) How could the psychologist in the above experiment do a better job of explaining exactly what type of sexual interactions he was observing?
2) What kind of descriptive observation is this? What is another name for this type of research?
3) Can you think of some other reasons why the female voles would increase/decrease these behaviors in the above experiment?
4) What would be the best way to determine whether it is nutrition that changes sexual behaviors? What type of validity does the above study lack?
5) What types of bias could the experimenter be introducing above?
6) Is this study worthless? If not, what are its advantages?

(II)   From the *psychology in action* portion of your text, it is suggested that you create a memory ethogram (see page 98). Suppose you did create an ethogram on prospective memory. At first you recorded your best friend's forgetting to get an idea of how this worked. You find that your best friend has more problems with prospective memory while under stress such as during exam time. After completing your analysis of your best friend and detailing his/her forgetting you then decide to examine whether exam stress decreases prospective memory in all students.

1) What type of study was the first analysis on your best friend's forgetting? What type of study is the analysis of other students?
2) Of the four types of descriptive observation listed in the text, which would you choose to complete this study? Why?
3) What types of problems could you encounter when trying to conduct this experiment?

(III)   A psychologist examines the motivational effects of cocaine in rats. She records how much rats are willing to press a lever to get cocaine. She finds that rats that have previously been given cocaine press a lever more often to get additional cocaine. She concludes that these rats love this drug and are pressing the lever more because they want to get high.

1) Is the experimenter anthropomorphizing in this experiment?
2) Can you think of reasons why the rats are pressing the lever more frequently other than the experimenter's conclusion that they want to get high?

3) Discuss the ecological validity of this experiment.
4) If the experimenter wanted to conduct a study on rat motivation with more ecological validity than this one, how might she go about this?
5) Is this study worthless? Why or why not?

(IV)   Several years ago, television ratings were determined quite differently than they are today. A carefully constructed stratified sample of households with television sets were provided with meters that were attached to the TV sets and recorded when the sets were on, and which station sets were tuned to. Why was this practice abandoned?

ANSWER KEY
Key Term Matching
1. c, b, d, f, a, e
2. d, a, c, e, b
3. b, d, e, g, h, c

Fill in the Blank
1.   naturalistic observations, case study, survey (pp. 89-91)
2.   database (p. 91)
3.   related (p. 91)
4.   reproduced (p. 101)
5.   ethology (p. 92)
6.   ethogram (p. 92)
7.   interobserver reliability (p. 93)
8.   case study (p. 89)
9.   deviant-case analysis (p. 96)
10. survey (p. 97)
11. anthropomorphism (p. 101)
12. reactive (p. 102)
13. observations, measurements (pp. 102-103)
14. indirect (p. 103)
15. participant observation (p. 103)
16. retrospective (p. 104)
17. motivated forgetting (p. 104)
18. style, response (p. 105)
19. social desirability (p. 105)
20. volunteer problem (p. 105)

Multiple Choice
1. c (p. 98)
2. a (p. 92)
3. a (p. 89)

4. d (p. 96)
5. b (pp. 97, 107)
6. a (p. 101)

48

7. a (p. 99)   12. c (p. 102)
8. b (p. 103)   13. b (p. 103)
9. d (p. 104)   14. c (p. 105)
10. c (p. 105)   15. b (p. 105)
11. a (p. 105)

True or False
1. F (p. 89)   6. F (p. 101)
2. F (p. 89)   7. F (p. 101)
3. T (p. 91)   8. T (p.97)
4. T (p. 92)
5. T (p. 99)

Experimental Dilemmas
(I)

1) He could create an ethogram to describe exactly which behaviors he was scoring as sexual.
2) a)Naturalistic Observation; b) ethology
3) For example, weather/temperature could have played a role, perhaps water not nutrition affects these behaviors, possibly the voles in the two different areas are genetically different and always display different sexual behaviors, perhaps it was the males who were not initiating sexual encounters. Can you think of others?
4) a) A true laboratory experiment where you can control for ALL other variables and only manipulate nutrition levels. b) The above experiment lacks internal validity; it does not demonstrate a true cause-effect relationship.
5) Participant reactivity (the voles may behave differently with him watching – wouldn't you?)
6) This study is not worthless, it provides new data to show that this is an interesting phenomenon occurring in the wild that merits further study.

(II)

1) a) Case study; b) Could be a survey or naturalistic observation.
2) There is no correct answer to this question. You could hand out a survey where students answer questions about their prospective memories or you could conduct naturalistic observation where you follow students around and record things they forget. Which of these would be easier? There are pros and cons to each approach, can you explain what they are?
3) From the text, there are several problems you could encounter. volunteer problem, subject roles, reactivity, social desirability. Can you think of others?

1) Yes, the experimenter suggests that these rats want to get high, this desire to get high is a human attribute, we don't know if rats are really enjoying the drug.
2) Perhaps the rats have developed an addiction to cocaine from their previous exposure. Thus rats are taking cocaine in this case because of their desire to avoid the negative effects of cocaine withdrawal rather than the positive effects of getting high. On the other hand, perhaps cocaine makes the rats hyper and it makes them press a lever more. Actually, these are both issues that people who conduct drug abuse research have to contend with! Can you think of other reasons why the rats lever press for cocaine?
3) There is no ecological validity to this study. Rats don't take cocaine in the wild!
4) The researcher may wish to study rat motivation by having them lever press for food or for sex.
5) This study is not worthless, while it lacks ecological validity, it can help us understand the mechanisms in the mammalian brain responsible for drug addiction.

(IV) Merely having a ratings meter in the household influenced how people watched TV. Thus, the data suffered from participant reactivity.

FURTHER READINGS
For a critical discussion on observational research and participant reactivity see:

Harris, F.C. & Lahey, B.B. (1982). Subject reactivity in direct observational assessment: A review and critical analysis. *Clinical Psychology Review.* 2(4), 523-538.

Sometimes it is helpful to read studies using particular designs. The following studies are case studies dealing with agnosia. Agnosia is the inability to recognize and identify objects or people despite having knowledge about the objects or people and no visual deficits. More information about agnosia can be found at http://www.ninds.nih.gov/disorders/agnosia/agnosia.htm.

Hattiangadi, Nina; Pillion, Joseph P; Slomine, Beth; Christensen, James; Trovato, Melissa K; Speedie, Lynn J. Characteristics of auditory **agnosia** in a child with severe traumatic brain injury: A case report. [References]. [Peer Reviewed Journal] *Brain & Language. Vol 92(1) Jan 2005, 12-25.*

Delvenne, Jean-Francois; Seron, Xavier; Coyette, Francoise; Rossion, Bruno. Evidence for perceptual deficits in associative visual (prosop)**agnosia**: A single-case study. [References]. [Peer Reviewed Journal] *Neuropsychologia. Vol 42(5) 2004, 597-612*

Web Resources

This page summarizes one major research project for the National Organization for Research at the University of Chicago, to archive and evaluate reliability for the November 2000 presidential ballot count from the state of Florida. The site should prove particularly useful to students as a demonstration of problems (e.g., variability in data coding) that are associated with observational methods. A detailed description of methods is included, including how measures of interobserver reliability were obtained (http://www.norc.org/fl/index.asp).

A number of Research Methods Tutorials can be found at Bill Trochim's (Cornell University) Center for Social Research Methods. Specifically related to this chapter is the tutorial on Observational Field Research (http://www.socialresearchmethods.net/tutorial/tutorial.htm).

The following URL is to SALMON (study and learning materials on-line) at the University of Plymouth. This site contains case studies in evolutionary psychology and ethology. Topics covered in the case studies include family life, toy design, and models of ethology for both animals and humans.
http://www.psy.plym.ac.uk/year2/psy225/Psy225.htm

There is a 20 page tutorial from StatPac on designing surveys and questionnaires which can be downloaded for free from:
http://www.statpac.com/surveys/

RESEARCH METHODS WORKSHOPS

Several workshop tutorials are related to this chapter. There is a general tutorial on *Surveys* and a second on *Designing a Survey* that addresses the importance of the sequencing and structuring of survey items as well as the importance of the visual appearance. A third tutorial (*Operational Definitions*) focuses on recording data from observational research. Wadsworth's *Research Methods Workshops* can be found at: http://psychology.wadsworth.com/workshops/.

Chapter 5

Relational Research

SUMMARY

1. Contingency Table Research
   1.1. **a contingency table** consists of two or more rows and two or more columns, where each row represents a category of one variable, and each column is a category of another variable
   1.2. **a cell** is a combination of a row category and a column category
   1.3. a contingency table shows how many observations fall into each cell
   1.4. contingency tables are usually analyzed with the χ^2 test for independence
       1.4.1. if the value of χ^2 is statistically significant, we can be reasonably sure that the two variables are related
   1.5. contingency table research is most often used with nominal level measurements
   1.6. subject reactivity can be a problem with contingency table research
2. Correlational Research
   2.1. **correlational research** examines the degree to which two variables are related and the direction of that relationship
   2.2. the correlation coefficient
       2.2.1. ranges from -1.0 through 0.0 to +1.0
       2.2.2. the *magnitude* of the coefficient indicates the strength of the relationship
       2.2.3. the *sign* of the of the coefficient indicates the direction of the relationship
           2.2.3.1. positive values indicate positive relationships; as scores on one variable increase, so do scores on the other variable
           2.2.3.2. negative values indicate negative relationships; high scores on one variable tend to be associated with low scores on the other
       2.2.4. the most commonly used correlation coefficient is **Pearson's product-moment correlation coefficient**, or **Pearson's *r***
       2.2.5. **scatter diagrams** are graphs that plot one variable on the abscissa, the other on the ordinate
           2.2.5.1. an individual is represented by a point that shows his or her scores on both variables
       2.2.6. interpreting correlation coefficients
           2.2.6.1. correlations do *not* imply a causative relationship between the two variables
           2.2.6.2. if A and B are correlated, we cannot tell whether A caused B, B caused A, or if both A and B were caused by a third variable
       2.2.7. low correlations: a caution

2.2.7.1. a **truncated range** of values on one or both of the variables

2.2.7.2. using *r* to measure a relationship that is not linear

2.2.8. reactivity in correlational research

2.2.8.1. reactivity may increase in correlational research as the number of measures increase since multiple measures provide additional cues regarding the purpose of the study

2.3. regression

2.3.1. **regression** is a statistical procedure for predicting the score on one variable based on the score of another (e.g., predicting college GPA based on SAT scores)

2.3.1.1. when multiple variables are used to make the prediction **multiple regression** is required (e.g., predicting college GPA based on SAT scores, high school GPA, and letters of recommendation)

2.3.1.2. **covariate** is a variable the researcher wants to control because it could also influence the outcome or prediction

2.4. complex correlational procedures

2.4.1. the internal validity of correlational research can be enhanced by examining *patterns* of correlations

2.4.2. the **cross-lagged-panel correlation procedure** obtains several correlations over time and considers the size and direction of the in order to determine likely causal relationships

2.5. experimentation and internal validity

2.5.1. experimentation involves the manipulation of an independent variable

2.5.2. the manipulation allows us to know the direction of the relationship between dependent and independent variables

2.5.3. if we know the direction of the relationship, we can identify the **proximal causes**, or the immediate causes of a behavioral event

LEARNING THE TERMINOLOGY

Cell. An entry in a data table defined by a particular row/column combination (p. 111). Any box in a table.

Contingency table. A relational research design in which the frequencies of all combinations of two variables are assessed to determine the relationship between them (p. 111). Table 5-2 contained on page 113 of the main text.

Correlation coefficient. A number that can vary from −1.00 to +1.00 and indicates the degree of relation between the two variables (p. 114). The positive correlation between smoking and lung cancer is reported to be high with numbers ranging from +.6 to +.7.

Correlational research. Relational research that shows both the degree and the direction of the relationship between two variables (p. 114). Research that is not experimental, does not prove causation but merely shows an association between two variables such as smoking and grades in college.

Cross-lagged panel correlation procedure. Calculating several correlation coefficients across time on the same participants to increase the internal validity of correlational research (p. 123). Measuring the correlation between two variables at two different time points and then all possible correlations in between to get a more accurate idea of these relationships.

Ex-post facto. Literally, "after the fact"; refers to conditions in an experiment that are not determined prior to the experiment , but only after some manipulation has occurred naturally (p. 111). Collecting data on college majors from a university after the majors have already been declared to eliminate participant reactivity from a survey or interview.

Pearson's product moment correlation coefficient. One form of correlation coefficient (p. 115). The number between +1 and −1 used to establish the degree of correlation.

Proximate cause. The immediate cause of an event, such as the independent variable in an experiment (p. 127). When we visualize something while trying to remember it, we remember it better. The proximate cause of increased memory in such a case is the act of using imagery whereas the ultimate cause may be evolution determining how we remember.

Regression. A procedure that uses a correlation coefficient to predict changes along one variable as a function of changes along one or more other variables (p. 121).

Relational research. Research that tries to determine how two or more observations are related (p. 111). Research that assesses how two variables are associated but is unable to determine if one causes the other, such as watching violent TV and aggressive behavior.

Scatter diagrams. A graphical relationship indicating degree of correlation between two variables made by plotting the scores of individuals on two variables (p. 116). Figure 5-1 on page 116 of the main text.

Truncated range. A problem in interpreting low correlations; the amount of dispersion (or range) of scores on one variable may be small, thus leading to the low correlation found (p. 119). In a college with high admission standards, the correlation between SAT scores and college GPA may be low, because only students with the top SAT scores are admitted and thus there is a truncated range of SAT scores.

Ultimate cause. The basic or final cause of an event, such as a "big bang" or evolution; *contrast with proximate cause* (p. 127). When we visualize something while trying to remember it, we remember it better. The proximate cause of increased memory in such a case is the act of using imagery whereas the ultimate cause may be evolution determining how we remember.

χ^2 **test for independence.** A test that is often used to determine the statistical significance of the relationship between variables in a contingency table (p. 112). You could use this statistic to determine if college majors are statistically different between males and females in a contingency table.

KEY TERM MATCHING

1.	
___contingency table	a. allows researcher to determined both the degree and direction of a relationship
___correlational research	b. data are collected after the fact of whatever produced them
___ex post facto	c. immediate causes of a behavioral effect
___proximal causes	d. includes both contingency table and correlational research
___relational research	e. shows how often observations fall in each category combination
2.	
___χ^2 text for independence	a. graphical means of portraying correlational data
___cell	b. entry in a data table
___correlation coefficient	c. measures the strength and direction of a relationship
___cross-lagged panel	d. one reason why r might be artificially low
___Pearson r	e. patterns of correlations are examined over time
___scatter diagram	f. the most common correlation coefficient
___truncated range	g. used to analyze contingency tables

FILL IN THE BLANK

1. _____ _____ attempts to determine how two variables are related.

2. _____ _____ are often used to determine whether two nominal variables are related.

3. In a contingency table, a _____ refers to a combination of a row variable category and a column variable category

4. Contingency tables show the _____ with which observations fall into each cell.

5. The _____ test for _____ is often used to analyze contingency table data.

6. In correlational research, both the _____ and the _____ of a relationship can be determined.

7. Relational research uses a _____ _____ to indicate the degree of relationship between two variables.

8. If two variables are related, we can use knowledge of one variable to _____ the other.

9. Most measures of correlation range in value from _____ to _____.

10. The larger the absolute value of the correlation coefficient, the _____ the relationship.

11. The sign of the correlation coefficient tells us the _____ of the relationship between two variables.

12. A _____ _____ is a kind of graph commonly used to present correlational data.

13. We are not entitled to infer a _____ relationship between two variables, solely on the basis of correlational evidence.

14. The reason that variable A is correlated with variable B might be that A is the cause of B, B is the cause of A, or that both A and B are caused by an unknown _____ _____.

15. Correlation coefficients may be artificially _____ if the range of either variable is restricted.

16. The use of the _____-_____-_____ correlational procedure provides greater internal validity than is provided by the traditional correlational approach.

17. In principle, _____ observation allows us to infer causality, because by manipulating the independent variable, and holding other variables constant, we know the direction of the effect.

MULTIPLE CHOICE

1. Relational research is undertaken to
   a. determine proximal causes.
   b. determine ultimate causes.
   c. identify how variables are related.
   d. explain one variable in terms of another.

2. Contingency table research is usually carried out when the data are
   a. nominal
   b. ordinal
   c. interval
   d. ratio

3. A contingency table must have at least ____ row(s) and ____ columns.
   a. 1, 1
   b. 1, 2
   c. 2, 1
   d. 2, 2

4. The various rows in a contingency table represent
   a. different variables.
   b. different categories of the same variable.
   c. different categories of different variables.
   d. relative frequencies of observations.

5. The rows and columns of a contingency table
   a. are different variables.
   b. are different categories of the same variable.
   c. must be the same in number.
   d. must be different in number.

6. Data in a contingency table are usually analyzed with a
   a. χ^2 test for independence
   b. χ^2 test for dependence
   c. Pearson r
   d. correlation coefficient.

7. The use of correlational techniques permits the researcher to
   a. make predictions on the basis of the obtained results.
   b. understand why two variables are related.
   c. manipulate the effect of one variable on another.
   d. infer a lack of causation.

8. Which variable are you most likely to see in a relational study with human participants rather than directly manipulated in an experiment?
   a. task complexity
   b. socioeconomic status
   c. intensity of a light
   d. Galvanic skin response

9. When r is positive
   a. low scores on one variable tend to go with low scores on the other
   b. high scores on one variable tend to go with low scores on the other
   c. low and high scores on one variable tend to go with low scores on another.
   d. low and high scores on one variable tend to go with high scores on the other

10. When r is negative
    a. high scores on one variable tend to go with high scores on the other
    b. high scores on one variable tend to go with low scores on the other
    c. low and high scores on one variable tend to go with low scores on another
    d. low and high scores on one variable tend to go with high scores on the other

11. Which of the following is an example of a positive correlation?
    a. head size increase as IQ increases
    b. IQ decreases as head size increases
    c. IQ stays the same as head size increases
    d. head size stays the same as IQ increases

12. Which of the following is an example of a negative correlation?
    a. head size increase as IQ increases
    b. IQ decreases as head size increases
    c. IQ stays the same as head size increases
    d. head size stays the same as IQ increases

13. When there is a strong positive relationship
    a. r is just less than 0.0.
    b. r is just more than -1.0.
    c. r is just more than 0.0.
    d. r is just less than 1.0.

14. When there is a weak positive relationship
    a. r is just less than 0.0.
    b. r is just more than -1.0.
    c. r is just more than 0.0.
    d. r is just less than 1.0.

15. When there is a strong negative relationship
    a. r is just less than 0.0.
    b. r is just more than -1.0.
    c. r is just more than 0.0.
    d. r is just less than 1.0.

TRUE FALSE
1. In principle, correlations permit causal statements.
2. Pearson's r is often used to analyze contingency tables.
3. Contingency tables usually are used with nominal data.
4. Reactivity can be a problem with ex post facto research.
5. Correlation coefficients usually range from 0.0 to 1.0.
6. Positive values of the correlation coefficient indicate stronger relationships than negative values.
7. A low correlation between variables A and B is proof that neither variable caused the other.
8. If an unknown third variable caused both variables A and B, the correlation coefficient would be smaller than if A caused B or vice versa.
9. Psychology, as all sciences, is concerned with demonstrating ultimate causes for the events in the real world.
10. Correlations should always be evaluated using the Pearson's product-moment correlation coefficient.
11. A contingency table is not an appropriate type of research when people are repeatedly measured on a task.

EXPERIMENTAL DILEMMAS
(I) A psychologist is interested in whether singing and talking to an infant will increase intelligence later on in life. He decided to have mothers record the amount of time they spent singing or talking to their baby during the first 4 months of life. Then he later gave the children an IQ test once they had entered school. His results were $r = +0.8$.
    1) Was there an effect of singing/talking and later IQ? Describe the relationship.
    2) Could participant reactivity have affected this experiment? How?
    3) Does singing and talking to a baby make the child more intelligent? What does this experiment tell us?

(II) A student was asked to measure the relationship between two variables for a class project. He decided to measure the correlation between sitting up front or in the back of the class and grades on the midterm. He presented the shown scatter plot and wrote that sitting up in front of the class is highly correlated with getting good grades on the exam. He reported a correlation of +1.0 for his data.

1) The professor gave him a zero for the project claiming he didn't really conduct a correlation coefficient. Why?

2) Can you think of other variables that may be causally responsible for the relationship between these two variables shown in the plot?

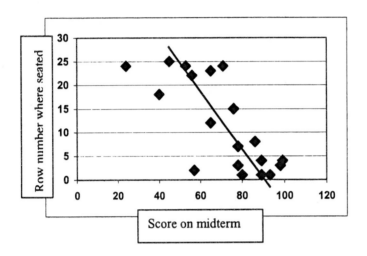

(III) An industrial psychologist interested in the effects of a work training program on job performance reported the following study. Fifty garment factory workers were given on the job training in a program that lasted either one or two weeks. Afterward their performance in terms of number of work pieces completed in one day was correlated with the number of weeks spent in training. The Pearson coefficient obtained between these two measures was –0.2. From this result the researcher concluded that the work training program was ineffective and should be abandoned. If you were a top management executive, would you comply with the researcher's suggestion? If not, why?

(IV) A social psychologist interested in the effects of unemployment on alcohol abuse conducted the following study. She mailed questionnaires to the homes of workers who had been laid off from a local automobile plant. The questionnaires were mailed at various time intervals and the workers were asked to fill them out anonymously and to return them. Fifty percent of the questionnaires were completed and returned. For those individuals who returned the questionnaires, the correlation between alcohol consumption and length of unemployment was found to be +.64. That is, more alcohol was consumed as the period of unemployment progressed. In her report the researcher stated that "the conditions of unemployment produce a tendency for people to increase their alcohol intake." If you were the journal reviewer deciding whether this work would be accepted for publication, what would your judgment be?

ANSWER KEY
Key Term Matching
1. e, a, b, c, d
2. g, b, c, e, f, a, d

Fill in the Blank
1. relational research (p. 111)
2. contingency tables (p. 111)
3. cell (p. 111)
4. frequency (p. 111)
5. chi square, independence (p. 112)
6. degree, direction (p. 114)
7. correlation coefficient (p. 114)
8. predict (p. 114)
9. −1.0, +1.0 (p. 114)
10. stronger (p. 114)
11. direction (p. 114)
12. scatter diagram (p. 116)
13. causal (p. 117)
14. third factor (p. 117)
15. lowered (p. 119)
16. cross, lagged, panel (p. 123)
17. experimental (p. 126)

Multiple Choice

1. c (p.111)	9. a (pp. 114-117)
2. a (p. 111)	10. b (pp. 114-116)
3. d (p. 111)	11. a (pp. 114-117)
4. c (pp. 111-112)	12. b (p. 115)
5. a (pp. 111-112)	13. d (pp. 114-117)
6. a (p. 112)	14. c (pp. 114-117)
7. a (p. 114)	15. b (pp. 114-117)
8. b (p. 111)	

True or False

1. F (p. 117)	7. F (pp. 119-120)
2. F (p. 115)	8. F (pp. 117-118)
3. T (p. 113)	9. T (p. 127)
4. T (p. 113)	10. F (p. 115)
5. F (p. 114)	11. T (p. 113)
6. F (p. 114)	

Experimental Dilemmas

(I)

1) There was a relationship between the number of hours singing/talking and later IQ. Showing a high positive correlation meaning that the more hours spent singing/talking, the higher the IQ observed.

2) Yes, anytime the data aren't collected ex post facto, participant reactivity is a possibility. Perhaps in this case, mothers knowing that their interactions with their babies were being monitored, they may have been having many more interactions with their babies when the researcher was not around to prove their baby would grow up smart.

3) This experiment only tells us that there is a relationship between the two. We cannot say that talking to a baby makes it smarter any more than we can say a high IQ in a baby makes mothers sing and talk. With correlations we must be careful not to infer causation.

(II)

1) From the graph we can see two things, first there is a negative correlation between the variables (the student reported a positive correlation). Secondly, the data points, while appearing to be correlated, are not perfectly correlated – they would have to all line up in a perfect line to have a correlation of 1. Thus, the correlation reported by the student was impossible from these data.

2) Students who are more dedicated to school tend to sit in the front of class and also study harder for better grades. Thus, the simple act of sitting in front of class may be helpful to learning, but it is unlikely to be the sole reason for increased grades.

(III)

No, because they only had two measures, one week or two weeks. Perhaps 5 days is enough training to increase productivity. They should have correlated productivity with more time points of training. This is an example of a truncated range.

(IV)

This work should not be published because the researcher is attempting to make a causative statement from her correlation. She simply observed a relationship between unemployment and drinking from a portion of the unemployed. It is as equally likely that alcoholics are less likely to obtain a job after being laid off than social drinkers. Remember that only half the people responded, they may be non-drinkers who promptly found another job.

FURTHER READINGS

For a review of the correlational research that has been conducted on college student alcohol consumption and its negative consequences see:

Perkins, H.W. (2002). Surveying the damage: A review of research on consequences of alcohol misuse in college populations. *Journal of Studies on Alcohol, Suppl.14*, 91-100.

The field of epidemiology (the study of factors that influence the occurrence and prevention of diseases) typically conducts relational research. Thus, establishing causation is often problematic in this area of study. The following review article discusses some of the hurdles and cautions from drawing causative conclusions from relational research.

Parascandola, M., Weed, D. L. (2001). Causation in epidemiology. *Journal of Epidemiology & Community Health, 55*, 905-912.

Thompson et al (2005) provide an excellent discussion on evaluating correlational research and how to improve our understanding of the relationship between two variables.

Thompson, B. E., Diamond, K. E., McWilliam, R., Snyder, P., & Snyder, S. W. (2005). Evaluating the quality of evidence from correlational research for evidenced-based practice. *Exceptional Children, 71*, 181-194.
[also available online at
http://journals.sped.org/EC/Archive_Articles/VOLUME71NUMBER2Winter2005_EC_Thompson71-2b.pdf]

WEB RESOURCES
For a thorough, and sometimes entertaining, summary of some "spurious correlations". This site demonstrates that correlation does not indicate causation:
http://www.burns.com/wcbspurcorl.htm

This page, developed by physicist Tom Kirkman of the College of Saint Benedict and Saint John's University, provides detailed information relating to graphical displays and the calculation of common statistics. Material relevant to Chapter 5 includes construction of contingency tables and the calculation of χ^2, as well as least square regression analyses. In addition to descriptive information, you may find use for the included on-line statistical calculators and graphical plotters.
http://www.physics.csbsju.edu/stats/

CyberLab has a section covering correlational design at:
http://faculty.frostburg.edu/mbradley/researchmethods.html#corr

Michael Taleff overviews surveys, case studies, and correlational research in an article for *Counselor Magazine*. The article provides a good review for the chapter and may be helpful while studying. You can find the article online at:
http://www.counselormagazine.com/pfv.asp?aid=revealing_the_lay_of_the_land.asp

Chapter 6

Basics of Experimentation

SUMMARY

1. What is an Experiment?
   1.1. experiments are tests designed determine causal relationships
   1.2. John Stuart Mill defined conditions for determining causation
      1.2.1. causality can be inferred if a result R follows some event E, and E and R vary together
      1.2.2. Mill also stated that causality can be demonstrated only with the **joint method of agreement and difference**.
         1.2.2.1. if E happens, R occurs (method of agreement)
         1.2.2.2. if E doesn't happen, neither does R (method of difference)
   1.3. The hallmark of an experiment is the production of a *comparison* by controlling the occurrence of an event, holding other aspects *constant*, and observing the outcome that was *produced*.
2. Advantages of Experimentation
   2.1. variables in experiments
      2.1.1. independent variable(s)
      2.1.2. dependent variable(s)
      2.1.3. control variable(s)
   2.2. groups in experiments
      2.2.1. **experimental group** receives the important level of the independent variable
      2.2.2. **control group** receives a comparison level of the independent variable
   2.3. experiments are often more ethical, more economical, and better controlled than alternative research procedures
      2.3.1. alternative to direct manipulation of the independent variable is **ex post facto** research in which participants are selected after the fact (quasi-experiment)
3. Variables in Experimentation
   3.1. **independent variables** are those manipulated by the experimenter
      3.1.1. **null results** - no demonstrated effect - may be obtained if inappropriate levels of the independent variable are selected.
   3.2. **dependent variables** are what the experimenter measures
      3.2.1. good dependent variables are
         3.2.1.1. reliable
         3.2.1.2. sensitive to differences in performance
         3.2.1.3. have an appropriate range of values in the experimental context to demonstrate the influence of the independent variable

3.2.1.3.1. **floor effects** exist when scores tend to be at the bottom of the scale

3.2.1.3.2. **ceiling effects** exist when scores tend to be at the top of the scale

3.3. **control variables** are potential independent variables that are held constant in an experiment.

    3.3.1. failure to control these variables leads to **confounding**, and makes the proper interpretation of the experimental results difficult or impossible

3.4. more that one independent variable

    3.4.1. most experiments include *more than one* independent variable

    3.4.2. combining variables is more efficient than doing several experiments and offers better experimental control

    3.4.3. **interactions** occur when the effects of one independent variable are not the same across all levels of another independent variable

3.5. more than one dependent variable

    3.5.1. several dependent variables may be appropriate for a given study

    3.5.2. economy suggests that as many dependent variables as feasible should be used in the same study

    3.5.3. most studies use only one or two dependent variables

        3.5.3.1. it is sometimes difficult to determine if multiple dependent variables are measuring the same thing

        3.5.3.2. difficult to statistically examine several dependent variables at the same time

4. Possible Sources of Experimental Error

4.1. **reactivity** in experimentation

    4.1.1. Experimental subjects have expectations about the nature of the experiment, and these expectations may modify their behavior (also referred to as **demand characteristics**)

    4.1.2. the **Hawthorne effect** is a classic example of the effect on behavior of being observed

        4.1.2.1. work productivity increased throughout the study regardless of the experimental manipulations

    4.1.3. Social roles have been identified that might influence behavior in a social setting

        4.1.3.1. a person with a **good-subject role** will do anything necessary to validate the experimental hypothesis

        4.1.3.2. a person with a **faithful-subject role** will attempt to be honest and faithful

        4.1.3.3. a person with a **negativistic-subject role** will attempt to sabotage the experiment

        4.1.3.4. a person with an **apprehensive-subject role** is uncomfortable about being evaluated in an experiment

            4.1.3.4.1. the **evaluation apprehension** leads to responding in a socially desirable way

4.1.4. Attempts to counter the effects of reactivity include
    4.1.4.1. doing **field research** (i.e. using unobtrusive measures in a natural setting)
    4.1.4.2. using **deception** to misdirect the subject as to the real purpose of the experiment
    4.1.4.3. withholding from the subject pertinent information about the study
    4.1.4.4. conducting **simulated experiments** in which subjects are ask to behave as if they were treated in a particular way
5. External Validity of the Research Procedure
  5.1. **participant/subject representativeness** refers to whether it is reasonable to generalize from the tested subjects to the population of interest (e.g., do results from college students generalize to all people)
    5.1.1. **reversibility** is a difficulty in establishing subject representativeness (e.g., disrupting a particular behavior by destroying a brain structure in one species does not necessarily mean that this structure controls the behavior in another species)
  5.2. **variable representativeness** refers to the extent to which we can generalize from the particular levels of an independent variable used in one study to other manipulations or levels of the independent variable
  5.3. **Setting Representativeness** refers to whether the testing situation has **ecological validity**, and whether the results can be generalized to the real world
    5.3.1. **(mundane) realism** refers to the degree to which an experimental situation is similar to those in the real world
      5.3.1.1. the focus of research is on psychological processes
      5.3.1.2. if the process is similar to that used in the real world then mundane realism is not a threat to validity
    5.3.2. **generalizability** refers to the ability to generalize findings from one setting to another can be established through field studies

Learning the Terminology

Apprehensive-subject role. A presumed role taken by a research subject who dislikes being evaluated (p. 152). A subject performing poorly in an experiment on reading ability simply because he/she is uncomfortable having his/her ability tested in the lab.

Ceiling effect. Difficulties in interpreting results when performance on the dependent variable is nearly perfect (p. 140). Testing math ability differences in subjects using a very easy math quiz would be difficult because everyone would do well.

Confounding. Simultaneous variation of a second variable with an independent variable of interest so that any effect on the dependent variable cannot be attributed with certainty to the independent variable; inherent in correlational research (p. 141). Inadvertently having one group contain all male and another contain all female subjects, thus the results of the experiment could be attributed to gender and not your independent variable.

Control. The technique of producing comparisons and holding other variables constant (pp. 135-136). Making sure that one group doesn't contain all male and another group doesn't contain all female subjects.

Control group. The group in a between-subjects experiment that receives a comparison level of the independent variable (p. 137). Having a group of subjects that receive a sugar pill when testing anti-depressant drugs.

Control variable. A potential independent variable that is held constant in an experiment (p. 140). Similar housing and feeding conditions for rats in different groups during the experiment.

Deception. A research technique in which the participant is misled about some aspect of the project; may be unethical. (p. 153). Milgram experiment where subjects were led to believe they were giving shocks to other people.

Demand characteristics. Those cues available to participants in an experiment that may enable them to determine the purpose of the experiment or what is expected by the experimenter (p. 150). Hawthorne effect.

Dependent variable. The variable measured and recorded by the experimenter (p.139). Score on a math quiz in an experiment on the effects of stress and math ability.

Ecological validity. The extent to which a research setting matches the environment of the problem under investigation; a threat to the external validity of experiments (p. 157). An experiment testing memory in a lab setting may not relate to natural memory and natural settings such as when a subject is sitting at home in his/her living room.

Evaluation apprehension. A source of reactivity in which participants are uneasy about being evaluated in an experiment. (p. 152). See Apprehensive-subject role.

Experiment. The systematic manipulation of some environment in order to observe the effect of this manipulation on behavior; a particular comparison is produced (p. 134).

Experimental group. The group in an experiment that receives the level of interest of the independent variable (p. 137). In an experiment on the effects of anti-depressants, the group of subjects that receive the drug rather than those who receive a sugar pill.

Ex post facto. Literally, " after the fact"; refers to conditions in an experiment that are not determined prior to the experiment, but only after some manipulation has occurred naturally (p. 138). Examining the relationship between gender and college major chosen would happen after the fact because you cannot pre-assign people to be male or female or which major to choose.

Faithful-subject role. When participants do their utmost to follow the demands of the experimenter. (p. 152). A subject who attempts to be faithful to the experiment he/she has some idea about its hypothesis.

Field research. Research conducted in natural settings in which subjects typically do not know that they are in an experiment (p. 152). Joining a cult to research social interactions of cult members.

Floor effect. Difficulties in interpreting results when performance on the dependent variable is either nearly perfect (a ceiling effect) or nearly lacking altogether (a floor effect) (p. 140). Testing math ability differences in subjects using a very challenging math quiz would be difficult because everyone would do poorly.

Generalizability. The issue of whether a particular experimental result will be obtained under different circumstances , such as with a different subject population or in a different experimental setting (p. 157). This can present a genuine problem with many psychology experiments which are tested on college students. Do college students represent the entire population on every psychological measure?

Good-subject role. When a subject attempts to determine the purposes of an experiment and reacts accordingly (p. 152). A subject in an experiment who tries to do poorly on a memory task after drinking caffeine because he/she guesses that the hypothesis is that caffeine impairs memory.

Hawthorne effect. Refers to conditions under which performance in an experiment is affected by the knowledge of participants that they are in an experiment (p. 150). Workers becoming more productive during an experiment testing worker productivity in response to many factors simply because they know they are being tested.

Independent variable. The variable manipulated by the experimenter. (p. 138). Whether or not subjects received stress in an experiment on stress and math ability.

Interaction. Experimental results that occurs when the effects of one independent variable depend on the levels of other independent variables (p. 144). The Piliavin , Piliavin and Rodin experiment with passengers on a New York subway described in the main text.

Joint method of agreement and difference. In Mill's system a situation, such as an experiment, in which X always follows A and never occurs when A is not present (p. 134). Tip-of-the-tongue experiment in main text.

Negativistic - subject role. When a participant deliberately attempts to sabotage an experiment (p. 152). A subject in an experiment on the effects of Ginko Biloba on memory enhancement who purposely does poorly on memory tasks to mess up the experiment.

Null results. Experimental outcomes where the dependent variable was not influenced by the independent variable (p.139). In an experiment on the effects of Ginko Biloba on memory enhancement, finding that Ginko has no effect on memory.

Realism. The extent to which a research procedure matches the characteristics of the real world; contrast with *generalizability* (p. 157). A lab experiment examining cocaine –seeking behavior in rats has little realism because rats in the wild don't take drugs.

Reversibility. An assumption made in research that the characteristics of different populations and species of subjects have the same underlying process; the behavioral "equation" can be determined form the behavior that is observed (p. 155). Simply because rats and humans will repeatedly take cocaine, it cannot be said that the same brain mechanisms control addiction in both species.

Setting representativeness. see *Ecological validity*

Simulated experiment. A fake experiment in which participants are told to simulate the behavior of real participants in a particular experiment (p. 154). In a study on hypnosis having one group simply pretend to be hypnotized to determine the reactivity factors.

Subject/participant representativeness. The degree to which research participants reflect the critical characteristics of other, more general populations, which will impact whether or not research results can effectively be argued to generalize (p. 155).

Type 2 error. Failure to reject the null hypothesis when it is in fact false (p.140). Having a statistical test determine that there is no difference between experimental groups when they are in fact different.

Variable representativeness. Determination of generality of results across different manipulations of an independent variable or different dependent variables (p. 156). If a researcher was interested in whether background noise decreases reading comprehension and tested this by comparing music to silence, it would be premature to assume that the results would generalize to all types of background noise unless music had variable representativeness to noise.

KEY TERM MATCHING

<table>
<tr>
<td>
1.
____apprehensive-subject role

____faithful-subject role

____good-subject role

____negativistic-subject role
</td>
<td>
a. suffers from evaluation apprehension
b. tries to be honest and faithful
c. tries to mess up the research
d. tries to validate the experimental hypothesis
</td>
</tr>
<tr>
<td>
2.
____ceiling effect

____ex post facto

____floor effect

____Hawthorne effect

____null results
</td>
<td>
a. classic example of participant reactivity
b. finding no effect of manipulating the independent variable
c. scores are clustered an the upper end of the scale
d. scores are clustered at the lower end of the scale
e. participants are grouped according to some characteristic not produced by the researcher
</td>
</tr>
<tr>
<td>
3.
____confounding

____interaction

____reversibility

____type 2 error
</td>
<td>
a. problem in establishing participant representativeness
b. failing to detect an actual treatment effect
c. when something unintended changes along with the experimental manipulation
d. when the effect of one independent variable depends on the level of a second independent variable
</td>
</tr>
<tr>
<td>
4.
____control

____control group

____control variable

____dependent variable
</td>
<td>
a. participants providing a comparison for the experimental treatment
b. participants receiving the level of interest of the independent variable
c. the essence of experimentation
d. what the experimenter holds constant
e. what the experimenter manipulates
</td>
</tr>
</table>

___experimental group ___independent variable	f. what the experimenter measures
5. ___deception ___experiment ___field research ___simulated experiment	a. an application of the joint method of agreement and difference b. research conducted in a natural setting c. study in which the participants pretend that they are receiving the experimental treatment d. when the participants do not know the actual purpose of the study
6. ___generalizability ___realism ___subject representativeness ___setting representativeness ___variable representativeness	a. ecological validity b. the appearance of naturalness of a research setting c. the extent to which experimental results can be said to be true d. the extent to which the independent variables and their levels represent conditions of interest in the real world e. the extent to which the participants tested represent the people in the population

FILL IN THE BLANK

1. The experiment of Brennen et al. was designed to determine whether a _____ or _____ was more important in relieving the tip-of-the-tongue state.
2. An experiment (such as Brennen's study) is designed to allow the researcher to find the _____ of a behavioral event.
3. One way that control is used in experimentation is that there is a control condition (or group) for purposes of _____.
4. Another form of control in experiments is that we can produce different levels of the _____ variables.
5. A final kind of experimental control is that we can control the _____ _____ and keep these factors constant.
6. The variable that is manipulated or varied is the _____ variable.
7. The events or behaviors that are observed and measured are the _____ variables.
8. Those aspects of the experiment that the researcher holds constant are called the _____ variables.

71

9. Those participants that receive the level of interest of the independent variable are referred to collectively as the _____ group.
10. The control group is comprised of participants who do not receive the important level of the _____ variable.
11. The major drawback in an ex post facto research project is that the researcher loses experimental _____.
12. When we select an independent variable we do so because we believe it will _____ behavior.
13. A failure of the independent variable to control behavior is sometimes referred to as a _____ _____.
14. If an independent variable is not an important factor in affecting behavior, then an experiment that employs this variable may produce _____ _____.
15. A failure to produce a strong manipulation of the _____ variable may lead to null results.
16. In order for a dependent variable to be useful it is important that the variable produces _____ data.
17. An unreliable dependent variable can often produce _____ results.
18. If performance levels (as measured by the dependent variable) are at the bottom of the measurement scale then this can result in a _____ effect. If performance levels are at the top of the scale then this can result in a _____ effect.
19. It is especially important to control extraneous factors when the magnitude of the effect produced by the independent variable is relatively _____.
20. The most direct experimental technique for controlling extraneous variation is to hold the variable(s) _____.
21. The likelihood of committing a Type 2 error (increases/decreases) _____ as we increase the sensitivity of the dependent variable.
22. It is (more/less) _____ efficient to conduct an experiment with three independent variables than to conduct three separate experiments.
23. If the same results are obtained across several independent variables then these results are said to be _____.
24. If the effects produced by one independent variable are not the same across the levels of a second independent variable this result is termed a(n) _____.
25. In an experiment employing only one independent variable it is not possible to obtain _____ effects.
26. Typically only _____ or _____ dependent variables are used in a single experiment.
27. A well known example of participant reaction is the _____ _____, named after a study in which industrial workers participated in a long experiment.
28. The Hawthorne effect represents one kind of _____.
29. A participant who adopts a _____ _____ role will do anything necessary to validate the experimental hypothesis.
30. Experiments conducted in natural settings suffer from the fact that the _____ that is characteristic of laboratory experiments may be lost in the natural environment.

31. _____ occurs when pertinent information is withheld from the participant.
32. The ability to generalize across different experimental manipulations is called _____
   _____.
33. _____ refers to whether the experimental setting bears a resemblance to the real
   world.
34. _____ is more important than _____ with respect to setting representativeness.
35. To test the generalizability of experimental results we might repeat the observations in a
   _____ _____.

MULTIPLE CHOICE

1. In Brennen's experiments on the tip-of-the-tongue (TOT) state, the independent variable
   was _____ and the dependent variable was _____.
   a. the cuing condition; percent of pictures identified
   b. the cuing condition; percent of TOTs resolved
   c. sex of the celebrity; percent of pictures identified
   d. sex of the celebrity; percent of TOTs resolved

2. The hallmark of an experiment is
   a. repeated positive correlations.
   b. repeated significant effects.
   c. producing a comparison by controlling the occurrence/nonoccurrence of a variable and
      observing the outcome.
   d. random assignment of subjects to conditions and tight procedural control over variables.

3. If two variables occur together in nature, then there is no control over the presumed cause.
   As a result this observation reveals
   a. correlations.
   b. causal relations.
   c. descriptive data.
   d. unreliable data.
   e. only strong relations.

4. In an experiment, the variable manipulated by the experimenter is the _____ variable and
   the behavior recorded by the experimenter is the _____ variable.
   a. independent; dependent
   b. dependent; independent
   c. observed; control
   d. control; observed

5. Dependent variables are dependent upon
   a. experimental manipulations.
   b. behavior of the subject.
   c. experimental control.
   d. comparisons produced experimentally.
   e. both a and b.

6. The variable manipulated by the experimenter in order to study its effect on behavior is called the
   a. control variable.
   b. experimental variable.
   c. dependent variable.
   d. independent variable.

7. In principle, experiments are designed to allow the researcher to make statements about
   a. causation.
   b. contiguity.
   c. correlation.
   d. strength of relations.

8. Null results can be caused by problems associated with the _____ variable(s).
   a. control
   b. independent
   c. dependent
   d. any of the above

9. A good dependent variable should be
   a. reliable.
   b. related to the independent variable.
   c. of theoretical interest.
   d. easy to observe.

10. Floor effects and ceiling effects result from using
    a. an unreliable dependent variable.
    b. only one level of the independent variable.
    c. two very extreme levels of the independent variable.
    d. a restricted range of the dependent variable.

11. A control variable is
    a. a potential dependent variable that is held constant.
    b. a potential independent variable that is held constant.
    c. a dependent variable that is varied in a controlled fashion by the experimenter.
    d. an independent variable that is varied in a controlled fashion by the experimenter.

74

12. Which of the following is NOT an advantage of manipulating several independent variables within the same experiment, as opposed to manipulating these variables in separate experiments?
   a. greater efficiency
   b. interaction effects may be observed
   c. control variables are more likely to be held constant
   d. results are easier to interpret
   e. all of the above are advantages

13. Which of the following is NOT one of the ways that control is used in an experiment?
   a. The control group is used as a basis of comparison.
   b. The independent variable is under controlled manipulation.
   c. The independent variable is directly controlled by the researcher.
   d. Extraneous variables are controlled by being held constant.
   e. All of the above represent ways in which control is used.

14. The "control" in control variable refers to
   a. the influence exerted on behavior.
   b. the fact that the experimenter must control the variable to ensure a valid comparison.
   c. the fact that the control group experiences the variable.
   d. the fact that the variable is subject to controlled manipulation in the experiment.
   e. the fact that the variable is under the direct control of the subject.

15. An interaction occurs when
   a. the effects produced by one independent variable are not the same at each level of a second independent variable.
   b. the effects produced by one level of an independent variable are not the same at other levels of that independent variable.
   c. the effects produced by an independent variable are not the same at each level of the dependent variable.
   d. the effects produced by a dependent variable are not the same at each level of the independent variable.

16. A valid experiment may produce null results because
   a. the levels of the independent variable are too similar to each other.
   b. the dependent variable is subject to a ceiling effect.
   c. extraneous variables are not held constant.
   d. all of the above

17. Which of the following fictional results is NOT an example of an interaction?
    a. with normally active children, the stimulating effect of amphetamines increases as the dosage increases, but with hyperactive children the greater the dosage of amphetamines, the calmer the children
    b. the level of humidity greatly affects people's comfort levels in the summer heat, but in the winter cold humidity levels make much less of a difference on comfort levels
    c. people who attend church regularly donate more money to charity than nonchurchgoers unless they are poor, in which case church attendance makes no difference
    d. children who watch violent TV shows are more aggressive than children who do not watch violent TV shows, although all children watch the same amount of TV
    e. college men go out drinking more often than college women, unless they are poor, in which case women go out drinking more often

18. The Hawthorne Effect is a classic example of
    a. participant reaction in an experiment.
    b. experimenter bias.
    c. field research using unobtrusive measures.
    d. mistakenly inferring causation from a correlation.

19. The Orne and Evans (1965) study involving asking subjects to perform dangerous acts demonstrates
    a. social conformity.
    b. a lack of ecological validity.
    c. unethical research.
    d. the volunteer problem.
    e. demand characteristics.

20. In a simulated experiment
    a. the demands of the situation are assumed to be the same for participants in all conditions.
    b. a laboratory experiment is replicated in an environment created to simulate the real world.
    c. there is greater ecological validity than in a laboratory experiment.
    d. None of the above

21. Ecological validity refers to the ability to generalize research finds to the _____ to which they are intended to apply.
    a. population
    b. people
    c. species
    d. environmental settings

22. Ecological validity is
    a. more dependent on generalizability than on surface realism.
    b. more dependent on surface realism than on generalizability.
    c. equally dependent on surface realism and generalizability.
    d. does not depend on either surface realism or on generalizability.

TRUE FALSE

1. Graessle et al found that rats given prenatal decompressions began to climb at a later age, and gained weight more slowly than controls.
2. The joint method of agreement and difference asserts that if a series of observations all agree on a specific ordering of two events then the first event must have caused the second event.
3. The joint method of agreement and difference requires pairs of observations made at the same time by the different observers.
4. The sole difference between the experimental group and the control group is that the former receives the independent variable whereas the later does not receive this variable.
5. Ex post facto research involves examining the aftereffects of the experimental manipulation employed by the researcher.
6. An important criterion for a good dependent variable is reliability.
7. When the dependent variable is restricted to a narrow range near the top of the scale of measurement this indicates a ceiling effect.
8. Experimental control is usually better in three experiments each employing one independent variable than it is in a single experiment employing three independent variables.
9. An interaction is obtained when the effect produced by one independent variable is not the same at different levels of another independent variable.
10. Whenever interaction effects are obtained it does not make sense to consider separately the effects of each independent variable involved in the interaction.
11. The Hawthorne Effect is a classic example of participant reactivity.
12. Field experiments maintain a higher level of control than is possible in a laboratory experiment.
13. If the results of a simulated experiment are highly similar to the results obtained with the independent variable, we can conclude that the independent variable effectively controls behavior.
14. Results concerning the operation of sensory processes in college students are very likely to generalize to other people.

EXPERIMENTAL DILEMMAS

(I) A researcher decides to conduct an experiment on the effects of pupil size on perception of attractiveness of faces. She compares male and female participants on their judgment of the level of attractiveness (using a Likert scale with 5 being least attractive and 5 being most attractive) of photographs of a wide range of men's and women's faces. The photographs have been retouched such that the faces of the same people are given to each subject, but some subjects view faces with large pupils, some with medium and some with small pupils. The results show that faces with large pupils are regarded as most attractive only when the photograph was of a face a female.

1) What were the independent and dependent variables in this study?
2) Was there a control group? Describe the control variables employed in this study
3) Was there an interaction?
4) If the experimenter had instead used photographs of models from a magazine, can you think of a potential reason why she might have obtained a null result?

(II) An industrial psychologist is contracted by a large manufacturing company that is having problems with employees arriving late for work. The psychologist first records number of times that employees arrive late during a one month period. He then introduces himself to the employees and interviews them about which sort of things they would like to see improved at work to make them happier. From the suggestions he chooses the most popular and economical suggestions (e.g. painting the walls a brighter color, allowing employees to bring in radios to be played at work etc.). He again records the number of times employees are late. He finds that employees are now arriving more promptly and shows the company a graph of his results. If you were the manager of that company, would you accept the psychologists findings? Why or why not?

ANSWER KEY
Key Term Matching
1. a, b, d, c
2. c, e, d, a, b
3. c, d, a, b
4. c, a, d, f, b, e
5. d, a, b, c
6. c, b, e, a, d

Fill in the Blank
1. picture, initials (pp. 132-133)
2. cause (pp.133-134)
3. comparison (pp. 135-137)
4. independent (p. 136)
5. environmental factors (p. 136)
6. independent (p. 138)
7. dependent (p. 139)
8. control (p. 140)
9. experimental (p.137)
10. independent (p. 137)

11. control (p. 138)
12. affect (p. 139)
13. null result (p. 139)
14. null results (p. 139)
15. independent (p. 139)
16. reliable (p. 139)
17. null (pp. 139-140)
18. floor, ceiling (p. 140)
19. small (p. 140)
20. constant (p. 141)
21. decrease (p. 140)
22. more (p. 144)
23. generalizable (p. 144)
24. interaction (p. 144)
25. interaction (pp. 144-146)
26. one, two (p. 148)
27. Hawthorne effect (p. 150)
28. reactivity (p. 150)
29. good subject (p. 152)
30. control (pp. 152-153)
31. deception (p. 153)
32. variable representativeness (p. 156)
33. realism (p. 157)
34. generalizability, realism (p. 159)
35. natural setting (p. 157)

Multiple Choice

1. b (pp. 132-133)	12. d (p. 144)
2. c (p. 135)	13. e (p. 136)
3. a (pp. 135-136)	14. b (p. 140)
4. a (p. 137)	15. a (p. 144)
5. e (p. 139)	16. d (pp. 139-141)
6. d (p. 138)	17. d (p. 144)
7. a (p. 134)	18. a (p. 150)
8. d (pp. 139-141)	19. e (p. 152)
9. a (p. 139)	20. a (p. 154)
10. d (p. 140)	21. d (p. 157)
11. b (p. 140)	22. a (p. 159)

True or False

1. T (p. 137)
2. F (pp. 134-135)
3. F (pp. 134-135)
4. F (p. 137)
5. F (p. 138)
6. T (p. 139)
7. T (p. 140)
8. F (p. 144)
9. T (p. 144)
10. T (p. 148)
11. T (p. 138)
12. F (p. 145)
13. F (p. 142)
14. T (p. 143)

Experimental Dilemmas

(I)

1) There are 2 independent variables: male vs. female faces and pupil size. The dependent variable is attractiveness on a scale of 1 to 5.
2) There was no control group per se. However, attractiveness of faces was controlled by presenting everyone with the same faces but with different pupil size.
3) There was an interaction; larges pupil size made faces more attractive only when the faces were female.
4) There may have been a null result because faces of models are all supposedly beautiful. Thus, perhaps all the faces would have been regarded as most attractive regardless of pupil size. This would have been a *ceiling effect*.

(II)

The findings should not be accepted because of *demand characteristics*. There are many reasons why the employees may now arriving on time, and it isn't necessarily because of the changes the psychologist made to the workplace. The Hawthorne effect, evaluation apprehension, and faithful-subject roles all potentially influenced the outcome of this study.

FURTHER READINGS

Ramón y Cajal (one of the first scientist to discover neurons in the brain) wrote a book on the exploration of science and basics of experimentation. Although the book was originally written over one hundred years ago, (English translation released in 1999) it is in some regards useful to the problems young scientists face today. This is a fascinating read!

Santiago Ramón y Cajal (1999). Advice for a Young Investigator. MA: MIT Press.

For those of you seeking a more relevant and current view on scientific experimentation.

Peter Medawar (1981). Advice to a Young Scientist. NY: Basic Books.

It might also be interesting the read G. Stanley Hall's (1885) article about the "new psychology" in which he discusses the current state of psychology at that time and how the field was advancing due to various experimental findings.

Hall. G. S. (1885). The new psychology, *Andover Review, 3*, 120-135, 239-248. [also available online (http://psychclassics.yorku.ca/topic.htm#experimental) at the Classics in the History of Psychology website developed by Christopher Green at the University of Toronto]

WEB RESOURCES
This page from Philip Zimbardo summarizes his classic (1971) social psychology experiment on imprisonment, where different Stanford University students were placed in the role of prisoner and guard for an extended period of time. The site represents a great example for discussions on experimental design, as well as on ecological validity (setting representativeness), realism, and generalizability. A detailed slide show is provided, along with some video and discussion items. http://www.prisonexp.org/

This web page by Mark Mitchell of Clarion University provides general lecture notes contrasting non-experimental and experimental methods. Discussed are issues of random assignment, statistical significance, and conclusions about research. A series of on-line quizzes is provided for students. http://psy1.clarion.edu/mm/General/Methods/Methods.html

Psychological Research on the Net is a website that catalogs known psychology studies being conducted online. You find it interesting to visit the site to see the variety of projects that are being conducted. You may also participate in the studies. Apart from helping someone in their own research efforts, we explore the different parts of experiments and how experiments differ from one area of psychology to another. http://psych.hanover.edu/Research/exponnet.html

RESEARCH METHODS WORKSHOPS
The *Manipulation Checks in Experimental Research* workshop defines the concept of a manipulation check and provides practice designing manipulation checks in sample experiments and a clinical trial. In addition, the *Experimental Methods* workshop distinguishes between experimental and non-experimental approaches and reviews general types of variables including independent, dependent, and subject variables (as well as quantitative and categorical variables). Confounds are also discussed. Wadsworth's *Research Methods Workshops* can be found at: http://psychology.wadsworth.com/workshops/.

Chapter 7

Validity and Reliability in Psychological Research

SUMMARY
1. Validity
    1.1. validity – a test or experiment measures what it is intended to measure (i.e., free of
          systematic error)
    1.2. predictive validity
          1.2.1. the idea that good measurements can predict other measurements
          1.2.2. example of the SAT I scores predicting GPA during first year of college
              1.2.2.1. in this example, GPA is the **criterion** measure and SAT I is the predictor
          1.2.3. calculated with a correlation coefficient
    1.3. **construct validity**
          1.3.1. the degree to which the independent and dependent variables measure what
                  they are intended to measure
          1.3.2. operational definitions and protocols help minimize construct invalidity
    1.4. **external validity**
          1.4.1. the degree to which the results of a study can be generalized to other
                  participants and settings
    1.5. **internal validity**
          1.5.1. the extent to which the results can be attributed to what was manipulated in
                  the study instead of some other variables (confounds) or design errors
2. Reliability
    2.1. reliability refers to the consistency of a measure
    2.2. types of reliability
          2.2.1. **test-retest reliability** is the ability of a measurement to provide the same
                  results when measured twice in a short period of time
              2.2.1.1. calculated with a correlation coefficient using
              2.2.1.2. **parallel forms** - different forms of the same test are compared
              2.2.1.3. **split-half** - a test is split into half (i.e., first half and second half or odd
                        and even items) and the two halves are compared
    2.3. statistical reliability and validity
          2.3.1. **statistical reliability** – likelihood results were not obtained by chance
          2.3.2. **sampling** influences the statistical reliability of measures, and therefore it is
                  important to conduct random sampling of subjects in an experiment
              2.3.2.1. **population**
              2.3.2.2. **sample**

2.3.2.3. **stratified sampling** – random samples taken from smaller units of the populations

3. Meta-Analysis
  3.1. **meta-analysis** is a statistical technique for summarizing findings across studies dealing with the same topic
    3.1.1. determines the validity of an observation across a large number of studies
    3.1.2. evaluates the size of the effect or strength of the observed effect
4. Measurement Procedures
  4.1. measurement is the systematic assigning of numbers or names to objects and the attributes of objects
    4.1.1. operational definitions
    4.1.2. intervening variables or **theoretical constructs**
    4.1.3. four measurement scales
      4.1.3.1. nominal (categorical data)
      4.1.3.2. ordinal (ranked data)
      4.1.3.3. interval (equal intervals)
      4.1.3.4. ratio (absolute zero)
    4.1.4. scaling
      4.1.4.1. psychophysical scaling assigns a value to a (well specified) physical input (e.g., brightness)
      4.1.4.2. psychometric scaling assigns a value to a (less well-specified) psychological input (e.g., depression)
  4.2. psychophysics
    4.2.1. applies psychophysical scales relating a psychological reaction to a physical event
    4.2.2. possibly represents the beginning of scientific psychology (Boring, 1950)
    4.2.3. **difference threshold** - the average difference in energy between stimuli that can be reliably distinguished (which is often measured to be half of the interval of uncertainty).
    4.2.4. Weber's law – the size of the difference threshold relative to the standard stimulus is a constant ($\Delta I/I = K$)
    4.2.5. **absolute threshold** - the average (minimal) amount of energy that is required for the detection of a stimulus
  4.3. psychometrics
    4.3.1. **summated rating scale**
      4.3.1.1. participants assign numeric values along a scale to reflect the degree to which they favor a particular interpretation of an object/event
      4.3.1.2. the ratings/points assigned to particular items are summed to obtain a score representing the psychological construct under investigation
      4.3.1.3. often referred to as **Likert scales**
    4.3.2. self-report methods
      4.3.2.1. most psychophysical and psychometric scales use self-report methods (i.e., personal reports by the participant)

4.3.2.2. lack immediate and direct corroboration sensitive to the wording of the measure

LEARNING THE TERMINOLOGY

Absolute threshold. The average point on a sensory continuum (such as light intensity) at which an observer detects a stimulus (p. 181). The lowest intensity of a tone which can be heard by a person.

Construct validity. The degree to which the independent variable and dependent variables accurately reflect or measure what they are supposed to measure (p. 165). Having subjects read out loud may be a measure of processes other than ability to read.

Criterion. An independent means of determining the validity of on observation, experiment, or judgment (p. 164). A criterion for the ability of SAT scores to predict college success is how well SAT scores predict GPA during the first year of college.

Difference. A basic property of all measurement scales, such that objects or their attributes can be categorized as different from each other (p. 178). Males are different from females.

Difference threshold. The average point at which two stimuli are judged to be different (half of the interval of uncertainty (p. 180). If you can only notice that a weight is heavier than another weight when it is 20 pounds or more heavier, then the difference threshold is 20 pounds.

Equal intervals. A property of measurement scales such that a one-unit change is equivalent throughout the range of the scale (p. 178).

External validity. Refers to the generality of research; externally valid research is representative of real life and does not distort the question under investigation (p. 167). In an experiment that establishes that math practice improves math ability in the lab, math practice should also improve math ability in subjects at home and at school.

Internal validity. Allows straightforward statements about causality; experiments are usually internally valid because the joint method of agreement and difference is employed (p. 168). In an experiment on math practice enhancing math ability the idea that increased math ability is caused by practice and not some other variable, such as attention from the experimenter.

Interval scale. A scale with equal intervals but without a true zero point (temperature in C or F) (p. 178). SAT scores .

Likert scale. see summated rating /Likert scale (p. 182). Asking subjects how much they like apple pie on a scale from 1 to 5, with one being not at all and 5 being very much.

Magnitude. A property of some scales of measurement that permits a determination of whether an item contains more, less, or the same amount of a given attribute (p. 178).

Measurement. The systematic assignment of numbers to objects or attributes of objects (p. 176). Measuring intelligence through an I.Q. scale.

Meta-analysis. A summary and (usually, a statistical) comparison of many research studies on a topic, often with the goal of addressing discrepancies in methods and/or outcomes (p. 174).

Nominal scale. A scale in which objects are named or categorized---the weakest measurement scale (p. 178). ZIP Code or university major.

Ordinal scale. A measurement scale in which objects or attributes are ordered but in which the intervals between points are not equal (p. 178). Placement in a beauty contest.

Parallel forms. Two alternative forms of a test (p. 171). Giving a subject a math test and then giving an alternate form of the math test a week later.

Population. The total set of population observations from which a sample is drawn (p. 172). All the students attending a university or all the people in a state.

Power. The probability of rejecting the null hypothesis in a statistical test when it is in fact false (p. 173). The ability of a statistical test to detect small differences between groups is increased when more subjects are tested.

Predictive validity. When a test can predict a particular outcome (p. 164). SAT scores and high school GPA have predictive validity for performance in university.

Psychometric scaling. Measurement of psychological concepts that do not have clearly specified inputs (p. 177). Depression scale.

Psychophysical scaling. Measures constructs that have well-specified inputs and outputs (p. 177). Loudness of a tone.

Psychophysics. Judgment of stimuli along a known physical dimension (p. 180). The perceived brightness of lights of different intensities.

Ratio scale. The highest form of scale in which there is a true zero and in which it is meaningful to consider multiplicative differences among attributes (p. 178). Percent of questions correct on an exam.

Reliability. Refers to the repeatability of an experimental result; inferential statistics provide an estimation of how likely it is that a finding is repeatable; also refers to the consistency of a test or measuring instrument determined by computing a correlation between scores obtained by participants taking the test twice (test-retest reliability). or taking two different parallel forms of the test, or scores obtained on each half of the test (split-half reliability) (p. 169). The idea that another scientist will get the same results if they carried out your experiment.

Replication. The repetition of an earlier experiment to duplicate (and perhaps extend) its findings; see also systematic replication (p. 168). The idea that if you repeated your experiment under different circumstances you would get the same results.

Sample. Observations selected from a population (p. 172). A portion of the population tested in an experiment such as a selection of students volunteering for an experiment from the general university population.

Self-report methods. Most psychometric scales and many psychophysical scales produce data based on a personal report by the respondent and not from observational measurements made directly by the researcher (p. 183). Asking a subject whether or not they can hear tones of differing loudness.

Split-half reliability. Determining reliability of a test by dividing the test items into two arbitrary groups and correlating the scores obtained on the two halves of the test (p. 171). Taking half the questions in a SAT exam and correlating them with the other half of the questions.

Statistical reliability. Rejecting the null hypothesis on the basis of a statistical test that yields an alpha level of less than .05 (p. 171). Showing that differences exist between groups based on inferential statistics.

Stratified sampling. A procedure where participants are selected to reflect the distribution (i.e., percentages) of one or more relevant characteristics in the general population in order to improve how representative the sample is of that population (p. 173).

Summated rating (Likert) scale. The sum of ratings given to attitude statements, on which people typically respond to positively- and negatively-orientated statements on five point scales (p. 182). Rating satisfaction with a professors performance based on a 5 point scale with 1 representing very dissatisfied and 5 very satisfied.

Test-retest reliability. Giving the same test twice in succession over a short interval to see if the scores are stable, or reliable; generally expressed as a correlation between scores on the tests (p. 171). Giving a group of people an I.Q. test two days in a row to see if the I.Q. test would produce the same results the second time.

Theoretical constructs. The idea that theory constructs the relationships along the numerous inputs and outputs that specify the intervening variables (pp. 176-177). The idea that intense light appears twice as bright and weak light appears dim maybe explained by the theoretical construct "brightness".

True zero. The absence of a physical property (zero weight in grams) as opposed to an arbitrary zero such as $0°$ Centigrade (p. 178).

Validity. Refers to whether an observation or procedure is sound or genuine (p. 164). Predicative, Construct, external and internal validity.

Weber's law Δ $1/1 = K$. The just-noticeable difference is a constant fraction of the base intensity (pp. 180-181). When a tone is twice as intense, we perceive it as twice as loud.

KEY TERM MATCHING

1.	
___construct validity ___external validity ___interobserver reliability ___internal validity ___validity	a. degree to which independent observers agree b. degree to which the observational environment is true of the real world c. degree to which variables accurately reflect what they are intended to measure d. degree to which we can be sure that experimental results are produced by the independent variable e. soundness or truth of observations
2.	
___operational definitions ___test-retest reliability ___replications ___split-half reliability ___confounding	a. help minimize construct invalidity resulting from error b. help assess the generality of the observations c. a major threat to internal validity d. refers to a high correlation between first and second scores obtained from a large sample e. refers to a high correlation between two parts of a test
3.	
___nominal scale ___ratio scale ___ordinal scale	a. placement in an Olympic event. b. body temperature in Kelvins c. hair color d. body temperature in centigrade

___interval scale	

FILL IN THE BLANK

1. The _____ of an observation refers to its truth.
2. _____ validity refers to the extent that a variable is an appropriate and accurate measure of whatever the variable represents.
3. _____ and _____ _____ are possible threats to construct validity.
4. An _____ _____ is a recipe that specifies how a construct is produced and measured in an experiment. Use of these helps to minimize _____ invalidity.
5. A _____ is a precise specification of how the measurement of behavior is to be undertaken.
6. _____ validity refers to the extent that research can be generalized to other settings and subject populations.
7. If we wanted to demonstrate that findings of a particular experiment had external validity, we should _____ the study under altered conditions.
8. The ability to claim that changes in behavior are caused by manipulation of the independent variable refers to _____ _____.
9. The major threat to internal validity is _____.
10. When a statistical test can detect small effects, it is said to have _____.
11. Random sampling means that each member of a population has a(n) _____ chance of being assigned to the sample.
12. A(n) _____ _____ is a group of subjects that is constructed to mirror the proportional membership in various categories that exists in the population.
13. A _____-_____ seeks to determine the external validity of a treatment by examining many research studies of that treatment.
14. Measurement is a systematic way of assigning _____ or _____ to objects or their attributes.
15. _____ involves the psychological reaction to physical events having a known dimension.
16. Another name for a summated rating scale is _____, so called after the person who developed it.
17. Many psychometric and psychophysical scales represent _____-_____ methods because the data come from what the respondent reports and not from observed behavior.

MULTIPLE CHOICE

1. Which of the following is NOT a form of validity?
   a. construct
   b. predictive
   c. statistical
   d. random

2. Whether SAT scores can estimate performance in college is an example of
   a. construct validity
   b. predictive validity
   c. external validity
   d. random validity

3. Variables that are considered confounding because they come from outside the bounds of a planned investigation are called
   a. external
   b. internal
   c. outlying
   d. extraneous

4. Which of the following is a threat specific to construct validity?
   a. lack of replication under different circumstances
   b. experimental setting
   c. apprehension by participants
   d. lack of one variable to predict outcome for another

5. The extent to which one can generalize from the research setting and participant population to other settings and populations is called
   a. predictive validity
   b. construct validity
   c. internal validity
   d. external validity

6. Confounding is the major threat to
   a. predictive validity
   b. construct validity
   c. internal validity
   d. external validity

7. Test reliability is NOT determined by
   a. matching method
   b. test-retest method
   c. parallel forms method
   d. split-half method

8. Zip code is an example of
   a. nominal scale
   b. ordinal scale
   c. interval scale
   d. ratio scale

9. Which of the following is an example of an interval scale?
   a. gender
   b. SAT scores
   c. placement in a race
   d. percent questions correct

10. A type of scaling used to measure constructs that have well specified inputs and outputs is called
    a. psychophysical
    b. psychometric
    c. interval
    d. ordinal

11. Which of the following is an example of psychophysical scaling
    a. depression
    b. intelligence
    c. brightness
    d. learning

12. According to Weber's law, the size of the difference threshold relative to the standard stimulus is
    a. constant
    b. increased
    c. decreased
    d. variable

13. According to Weber's law, if 2 decibels (dB) is the difference threshold for a 60 dB tone, and 4 dB is the difference threshold for a 120 dB tone, what would be the difference threshold for a 30 dB tone?
    a. 1
    b. 2
    c. 3
    d. 8

14. Most psychometric and many psychophysical scales represent self-report methods because
    a. the data come from the experimenters themselves
    b. the data come from behavior that is observed
    c. the data are untrustworthy
    d. the data come from a personal report by the respondent

15. A major concern with self-report is that they
    a. cannot be reported on a psychometric scale
    b. cannot be easily verified
    c. increase fatigue
    d. are notoriously unreliable

TRUE FALSE
1. Validity and invalidity refer to the best approximation to the truth or falsity of propositions.
2. Amount of hair, as a measure of intelligence, would seem to lack external validity.
3. Random error is a major threat to the internal validity of an observation.
4. Protocols are more precise than operational definitions.
5. Research findings that are only true of a particular strain of white rats would seem to lack predictive validity.
6. Construct validity can be demonstrated by replicating an experiment with different tasks.
7. In principle, experimental observations permit causal statements.
8. Imprecise protocols are the major threat to internal validity.
9. In a meta-analysis, the researcher carries out his/her own experiments.
10. Like other forms of descriptive observation, meta-analysis is a first step in understanding behavior.
11. Variability can be present in a group of measures even when they measure the same thing.

EXPERIMENTAL DILEMMAS

(I) Two psychologists decided to measure depression in the same population of patients. The first decided to measure the number of suicide attempts per year and the second measured it using a well established self-rating scale for depression which gives a measure between 40 and 100 with 40 being not at all depressed and 100 being most depressed.

1) What scale of measurement did each psychologist use (nominal, interval, ordinal or ratio)?

2) What would be another name for the scales used by the second psychologist?

3) Which system of measurement of the two in this example do you think is better? Why?

ANSWER KEY

Key Term Matching
1, c, b, a, d, e
2. a, d, b, e, c
3. c, b, a, d

Fill in the Blank
1. validity (p. 164)
2. construct (p. 165)
3. confounding, random errors (pp. 165-166)
4. operational definition, construct (p. 167)
5. protocol (p. 167)
6. external (p. 167)
7. replicate (p. 168)
8. internal validity (p. 168)
9. confounding (p. 168)
10. power (p. 173)
11. equal (p. 172)
12. stratified sample (p. 173)
13. meta-analysis (p. 174)
14. numbers, names (p. 176)
15. psychophysics (p. 180)
16. Likert scale (p. 182)
17. self-report (p. 183)

Multiple Choice
1. d (pp. 164-168, 171)
2. b (p. 164)
3. d (p. 165)
4. c (p. 166)
5. d (p. 167)
6. c (p. 168)

7. a (p. 171)   12. a (p. 180)
8. a (p. 178)   13. a (pp. 180-181)
9. b (p. 178)   14. d (p. 183)
10. a (p. 177)   15. b (p. 183)
11. c (p. 177)

True or False
1. T (p. 164)   7. T (p. 168)
2. F (p. 167)   8. F (p. 167)
3. F (p. 168)   9. F (p. 174)
4. T (p. 167)   10. F (p. 174)
5. F (p. 164)   11. T (pp. 176-177)
6. F (p. 167)

Experimental Dilemmas

(I)

1) The first psychologist used a ratio scale because number of suicide attempts has a meaningful zero. The second used an interval scale because the self-rating scale had an equal interval but not a meaningful zero.

2) Another name for this scale would be psychometric scaling using a self-report method.

3) There really is no better way, because it depends upon what question the experimenter is trying to answer. For example, number of suicide attempts is an observable and objective measure compared to a self-rating scale. However, the self-rating scale is probably more informative about the degree and subtype of depression.

FURTHER READINGS
For those interested in psychophysics methodology, there is a comprehensive review on how we measure taste and smell (olfaction).

Dalton, P. (2002). Olfaction. In H. Pashler, S. Yantis (Eds.), Steven's handbook of experimental psychology (3rd ed.), Vol. 1:Sensation and perception (pp. 691-746). New York, NY: John Wiley & Sons.

Pain is an area of research in perception but has also become an important area of applied research with chronically or terminally ill patients. The following chapter reviews the psychophysical foundation of pain research.

Price, D. D., Riley, J. L., Wade, J. B. (2001). Psychophysical approaches to measurement of the dimensions and stages of pain. In D. C. Turk & R. Melzack, Ronald (Eds), *Handbook of pain assessment,* 2nd ed. (pp. 53-75). New York: Guilford Press.

WEB RESOURCES

This particular demonstration gives students valuable hands-on experience with various psychophysical methods for determining threshold. The demonstration compares difference thresholds for line length judgments in the Müller-Lyer illusion for the methods of adjustment, limits, constant stimuli, plus adaptive procedures, along with a brief description of each method. Individual results from each method are displayed after the completion of the demonstration experiment.
http://www.psych.purdue.edu/~coglab/VisLab/initial.html

This site is the homepage for the International Society for Psychophysics, a group founded in 1985 to promote psychophysical research. A brief description of psychophysics is provided as well as psychophysical demonstrations.
http://www.uni-leipzig.de/~isp/isp/history/history.htm

A tutorial describing different types of validity and reliability and highlights the difference between validity and reliability is available at this site:
http://www.socialresearchmethods.net/tutorial/Colosi/lcolosi2.htm

The history of validity is outlined at:
http://suen.ed.psu.edu/~hsuen/Evolve.pdf

RESEARCH METHODS WORKSHOPS

Reliability and Validity distinguished between reliability and validity and defines various types of reliability along with the corresponding statistical analyses. *Sampling Methods* describes methods of obtaining appropriate samples so that results are valid and generalizable. Wadsworth's *Research Methods Workshops* can be found at:
http://psychology.wadsworth.com/workshops/.

Chapter 8

Experimental Design

SUMMARY
1. Internal Validity in Experiments
    1.1. In a properly designed experiment, behavioral effects result solely from manipulations of the independent variables. This means that experimental results are internally valid.
    1.2. executive monkeys
    1.3. experiments with LSD
2. Experimental Design
    2.1. between-subjects designs
        2.1.1.   each individual participant is assigned to one of the treatment conditions
        2.1.2.   there is no chance of one treatment condition contaminating another since each participant serves in only one condition
        2.1.3.   if the participants assigned to the different groups are not equivalent, participant differences are confounded with levels of the independent variable
        2.1.4.   matching and randomization (procedures for equating the groups)
            2.1.4.1. matching
                2.1.4.1.1.   sets of equivalent subject are identified, often using a pretest
                2.1.4.1.2.   one member of each set is randomly assigned to each treatment condition
                2.1.4.1.3.   experimenter cannot match on all relevant variables, and may not know what to match on
                2.1.4.1.4.   subject attrition, the loss of one or more participants from the study, will result in unequal groups
            2.1.4.2. randomization
                2.1.4.2.1.   subjects are assigned randomly to the various treatment conditions
                2.1.4.2.2.   this procedure is the preferred method of equating groups of participants, since each participant has an equal and unbiased chance of being in any treatment condition
    2.2. within-subjects designs
        2.2.1.   each participant is tested in every experimental condition
        2.2.2.   advantages of within-subjects designs include
            2.2.2.1. efficiency of research
            2.2.2.2. the treatment groups are guaranteed to be equivalent
        2.2.3.   carryover effects are a threat to the internal validity of experiments that use within-subjects designs
            2.2.3.1. **carryover effects** occur when the effects of being tested in one condition carry over and influence the behavior measured in another condition

2.2.3.2. carryover effects can be minimized by randomly determining the sequence of treatments received by different participants

2.2.3.3. using counterbalancing procedures to determine the order of treatments received by every participant

    2.2.3.3.1. **complete counterbalancing** requires that all possible orders of treatments be used for the same number of participants (impractical with a large number of treatments)

    2.2.3.3.2. **incomplete counterbalancing** presents each treatment equally often at each stage of the experiment

        2.2.3.3.2.1. **a Latin-square** design is a convenient way to generate the required treatment orders

        2.2.3.3.2.2. a balanced Latin square is a special kind of Latin square in which each treatment precedes and follows every other treatment equally often

3. Control Conditions

  3.1. control conditions in an experiment provide a baseline against to which the level in interest of the independent variable can be compared

  3.2. **mixed designs**

    3.2.1. are often appropriate for experiments with more than one independent variable

    3.2.2. some independent variables are tested between subjects and the others are tested within subjects

4. Choosing an Experimental Design

  4.1. carryover effects

    4.1.1. if an experimental treatment is likely to produce a permanent on long-lasting effect on participants a between-subjects design should be used

    4.1.2. a within-subjects design should be used to study changes in behavior over time

  4.2. individual differences

    4.2.1. refers to the various ways in which people are different from each other

    4.2.2. if large individual differences are likely to influence the dependent variable, a within-subjects design might be preferable to a between-subjects design

  4.3. contrasting between- and within-subjects designs

    4.3.1. must balance carryover effects and individual differences

    4.3.2. can do the study using both designs

        4.3.2.1. may lead to different results

        4.3.2.2. within-subject designs seem to be more sensitive to the effects of the independent variable

LEARNING THE TERMINOLOGY

Balanced Latin Square A counterbalancing scheme in which each condition is preceded and followed equally often by every other condition (p. 199). See tables 8-3 and 8-4 on pages 199-200.

Baseline The normal or typical behavior used as a standard of comparison in an experiment (p. 202). Determining eating habits of a person during several weeks prior to initiation of several therapies to change eating habits, to have a basis of comparison after therapy.

Between-subjects design An experimental design in which each subject is tested under only one level of each independent variable (p. 189). Assigning one group of subjects to one types of stress, another group to a second type of stress and then a final separate groups of subjects to a no stress control condition.

Carryover effects Relatively permanent effect that testing subjects in one condition has on their later behavior in another condition (p. 196). In an experiment that examines different types of visualization for sports performance, if you tested a subject using one type of visualization and then another, the first may have already taught the athlete better performance which will affect their performance following the second type of visualization.

Control condition The comparison condition in a within-subjects design; *compare to control group* (p. 201). In an experiment examining the effects of several types of stress, also having a condition with no stress as a basis of comparison.

Counterbalancing Refers to any technique used to vary systematically the order of conditions in an experiment to distribute the effects of time of testing (practice and fatigue) so they are not confounded with conditions (p. 192). Having half the subjects perform a task with no stress, and then again following stress, and having the other half of the subjects perform the task following stress and again at a later time with no stress.

Individual differences A problem that may confound the results of a between-subjects experiment (p. 204). Most people differ in their reaction to a drug, it may have profound effects on some and little or no effect on others.

Internal validity Allows straightforward statements about causality; experiments are usually internally valid because the joint method of agreement and difference is employed (p. 189). In an experiment on whether math practice enhances math ability, the idea that increased math ability is caused by practice and not some other variable, such as attention from the experimenter.

Latin-square design A counterbalancing procedure in which each conditioning occurs equally often during each time period of the experiment; *see balanced Latin square* (p. 198). Table 8-2 on page 198.

Matching Assigning subjects into groups based on some characteristic assumed to be correlated with the dependent variable (p. 194). Before beginning an experiment on the effects of math practice on math ability, assigning participants to each treatment such that the level of math ability in each treatment is the same. In other words, having the same number of participants who are really good at math in each treatment.

Randomization The process of unbiased assignment of subjects to conditions of unbiased variation of condition order (p. 195). Assigning a number to all the participants in a study and then having a random number generator select the numbers for the participants to be assigned to each treatment.

Subject attrition When a subject fails to complete an experiment (p. 195). Participants who drop out of an experiment because they become ill, move away, or perhaps decide they don't want to be in the experiment anymore.

Within-subjects design An experimental design in which each subject is tested under more than one level of the independent variable (p. 189). In an experiment on the effects of stress, having participants encounter one type of stress, then another type and also testing each participant when they have no stress.

KEY TERM MATCHING

1. ___ balanced Latin square ___ between-subjects design ___ Latin-square design ___ within-subjects design	a. each participant receives every treatment b. each participant receives only one treatment c. each treatment precedes and follows every other treatment equally often d. every treatment appears equally often at each stage in the experiment
2. ___ counterbalancing ___ matching ___ randomization	a. less preferred way of establishing equivalent groups b. preferred way of establishing equivalent groups c. used to minimize carryover effects
3. ___ control condition ___ individual differences ___ internal validity ___ subject attrition	a. provides a baseline for comparison with the treatment of interest b. why treatment groups may not be equivalent c. in principle, a property of the experimental method d. a problem, especially when matching is used to form equivalent groups

FILL-IN-THE-BLANK
1. A good experiment allows the researcher to state that changes in the independent variable _____ the observed changes in the dependent variable.
2. Experiments that lead to valid results are said to be _____ valid.

3. In the "executive monkey" experiments reported by Brady and his colleagues, the independent variable was (describe briefly) _____

4. Weiss (1971) showed that animals which respond at a _____ rate are likely to get ulcers, whether they are helpless or in control.

5. An experimental design in which each participant receives all levels of the independent variable is called a _____-subjects design.

6. The first design decision an experimenter must make is how to assign _____ to the various levels of the independent variable.

7. An experiment in which each participant is assigned to a particular level of the independent variable is called a _____-subjects design.

8. In any between-subjects experiment the researcher must strive to minimize differences among the _____ _____ that may exist before the experiment begins.

9. When the technique of matching is used to equate the various treatment groups the experimenter is trying to match on the basis of important _____ characteristics.

10. Matching is done on the basis of the most likely _____ variables.

11. When one or more of the participant s in an experiment do not complete the experiment this introduces the problem of subject _____.

12. The technique known as _____ is used to ensure the formation of equivalent groups of participants by giving each participant an equal opportunity to serve in any condition of the experiment.

13. Experimental design is concerned with the logic of _____ experiments.

14. The preferred technique for assigning participants to experimental conditions is the _____ technique.

15. The _____-subjects design is generally the more efficient design.

16. If participation in one treatment condition is likely to affect performance in another treatment condition, then we would say that _____ effects pose a problem in this experiment.

17. The problem with using randomization to minimize carry-over effects is that a large number of _____ are required.

18. Complete _____ ensures that all possible treatment orders are used.

19. In a balanced _____-_____ design every experimental condition is preceded and followed equally often by every other condition.

20. If two Latin squares were needed to counterbalance the order of treatment presentations, than there must have been a(n) _____ number of treatment conditions.

21. A _____ design is one that employs both within- and between-subjects variable.

22. In its simplest form, a _____ group is the group that does not receive the levels of interest of the independent variable.

23. A control condition provides a _____ against which some other variable of the experiment may be compared.

24. Suppose your independent variable is likely to exert a permanent effect on your participants. What type of design should you employ in this case? _____

25. What type of design should be employed if there are large individual differences among the participants in your sample? _____

MULTIPLE CHOICE

1. In principle, experiments are designed to allow statements about
   a. causation.
   b. contiguity.
   c. correlation.
   d. relatedness.
   e. both c and d

2. The results of the early "executive-monkey" studies were invalid because
   a. the shocks used to induce stress were themselves capable of producing ulcers.
   b. the subjects assigned to the "executive" and "co-worker" conditions were different even prior to the beginning of the experiment.
   c. it is not valid to compare directly the results of animal research and human behavior.
   d. the differences between the experimental and control groups reflect correlations and not true causal relations.

3. In a simple between-subjects experimental design, each participant is given _____ level of the independent variable; in a within-subjects design each participant is given _____ level of the independent variable.
   a. one; one
   b. each; one
   c. one; each
   d. each; each

4. The purpose of good experimental design is to
   a. minimize extraneous or uncontrolled variation.
   b. come up with interesting research ideas.
   c. increase the likelihood that an experiment will produce internally valid results.
   d. avoid carry-over effects.
   e. both a and c

5. Which of the following is not a problem associated with between-subjects designs?
   a. the between-subjects design is a conservative design
   b. carry-over effect
   c. unequal treatment groups prior to the introduction of the independent variable
   d. subject attrition

6. The difference between a within-subjects design and a between-subjects design is that
   a. fewer participants are needed in a between-subjects design.
   b. each participant serves as his or her own control in within-subject designs.
   c. confounding cannot occur with between-subjects designs.
   d. a given participant's behavior is measured only once in within-subjects designs.

7. A major disadvantage of between-subjects designs is that
   a.   the effect of one treatment may alter the effectiveness of later treatments.
   b.   participant differences may obscure treatment effects.
   c.   one must use fewer independent variable.
   d.   one can use only one dependent variable.

8. In order to obtain equivalent groups in between-subjects designs, you can
   a.   randomly assign participants to the various treatment groups.
   b.   use each participant as his or her own control.
   c.   attempt to match participants on variables that are relevant.
   d.   all of the above
   e.   both a and c

9. One reason for preferring randomization to matching for establishing group equivalence is that
   a.   we do not know all the relevant variables to match.
   b.   randomization involves less confounding.
   c.   counterbalancing does not require randomization.
   d.   randomization guarantees group equivalence.

10. For between-subjects designs, randomization and matching are techniques used in an attempt to
   a.   prevent treatment carry-over effects.
   b.   ensure that the groups are equivalent at the start of the experiment.
   c.   minimize experimenter effects.
   d.   minimize demand characteristics.
   e.   both c and d

11. In within-subjects designs, counterbalancing is used to
   a.   enable the experimenter to evaluate possible treatment order effects.
   b.   assign participants to treatment groups.
   c.   eliminate the effects of treatment order.
   d.   all of the above

12. In a completely counterbalanced experimental design
   a.   each group of participants receives a different treatment.
   b.   every participant receives every treatment.
   c.   all possible treatment orders are used.
   d.   the treatment orders are randomized.
   e.   both b and c

13. In a balanced Latin square design
    a. each treatment appears once in each row.
    b. each treatment appears once in each column.
    c. each treatment precedes and follows every other treatment equally often.
    d. all of the above
    e. both a and b

14. If a 6 x 6 balanced Latin square were used to determine the order of presentation of 6 treatment conditions, in what multiples would the experimenter have to test subjects in?
    a. 6
    b. 12
    c. 36
    d. 216

15. A mixed design is one in which
    a. there is one independent and one dependent variable.
    b. at least one independent variable is tested within-subjects and the other independent variable(s) is (are) tested between-subjects.
    c. one independent variable is manipulated and the other independent variable(s) is (are) controlled.
    d. each participant receives a mixture of treatment conditions.

16. A control group or a control condition is included in an experiment to
    a. evaluate experimenter effects and demand effects.
    b. provide a baseline against which the variable of interest can be compared.
    c. prevent ceiling or floor effects.
    d. increase the generalizability of the results.

17. In an experiment designed to investigate the effects of alcohol on appetite, if drinks X and Y contain 0.5 and 1.0 ounces of vodka in orange juice, respectively, and drink Z contains only orange juice then the control group in the experiment should receive
    a. drink X.
    b. drink Y.
    c. drink Z.
    d. nothing to drink.
    e. X, Y, and Z in a counterbalanced order.

TRUE-FALSE

1. Experiments are internally valid in principle.
2. A major concern in experimental design is preventing carryover effects in within-subjects designs.
3. The first design decision an experimenter must make is what levels of the independent variable should be used.
4. A within-subjects design is more conservative than a between-subjects design.

5. If an experimenter suspects that the effects of one treatment may linger on to alter behavior in a later condition, then she should use a counterbalanced within-subjects design.
6. The technique of counterbalancing is used in within-subjects designs to reduce the effects of treatment order.
7. One difficulty with matching is that the experimenter cannot know all the potentially relevant dimensions on which to match subjects.
8. Subject attrition has a less detrimental effect when group characteristics are determined by an unbiased procedure, as compared to a matching procedure.
9. Random assignment of subjects to conditions guarantees that treatment groups will be equal prior to the administration of the independent variable.
10. Within-subjects designs are generally more efficient than between-subjects designs.
11. Carry-over effects are eliminated in a completely counterbalanced design.
12. Unless the number of experimental conditions is greater than 7, a single balanced Latin square is sufficient for counterbalancing treatment orders within an experiment.
13. Counterbalancing can be used for assigning treatment orders as well as determining the order of testing when more than one independent variable is used.
14. The control group is the group that does not receive the levels of interest of the independent variable.

EXPERIMENTAL DILEMMA

A researcher is interested in studying the effect of environmental stress on the performance of various mental tasks. The environmental stressor is the temperature level in the experimental chamber. The researcher selects three different temperatures (40 F, 70 F, and 90 F) for the levels of stress to be included in the experiment. Since this is an experiment involving some risk to the participants, the researcher employs male undergraduates to serve as participants. The mental task selected for the first experiment is a choice reaction time task in which one of four stimulus lights comes on and the participant is to respond by pressing one of four buttons as quickly as possible. The researcher thinks that stressful environments will make participants respond faster.

The researcher tests each participant in each condition during the 90 minute testing session. Each participant is first tested in the 70 condition, then the 90 condition, and finally in the 40 condition. Participants receive 30 trials in each condition.

The results showed that the participants mean reaction times for the three conditions were as follows:

Temperature	Mean Reaction Time
40 F	430 msec
70 F	525 msec
90 F	487 msec

Statistical analysis of the mean reaction times revealed that each of the three conditions was reliably different from the other two conditions. The researcher concluded that thermal stress improves reaction time. Do you agree with this conclusion?

ANSWERS

Key Term Matching
1. c, b, d, a
2. c, a, b
3. a, b, c, d

Fill-in-the-Blank
1. cause (p.189)
2. internally (p. 189)
3. ability to postpone shock (p.189)
4. high (p. 190)
5. within (p. 189)
6. participants (p. 193)
7. between (p. 189)
8. treatment groups (p. 194)
9. participant (p. 194)
10. confounding (p. 154-155)
11. attrition (p. 194)
12. randomization (p. 195)
13. arranging (p. 195)
14. randomization; (p. 156)
15. within (p. 196)
16. carryover (p. 196)
17. participants (pp. 197-198)
18. counterbalancing (p. 197)
19. Latin square (p. 199)
20. odd (p. 200)
21. mixed (p. 203)
22. control (p. 201)
23. baseline (p. 202)
24. between-subjects (p. 203)
25. within-subjects (p. 204)

Multiple Choice
1. a (p. 189)
2. b (p. 190)
3. c (p. 189)
4. e (p. 193)
5. b (pp. 194-195)
6. b (pp. 193-194)
7. b ((p. 195)
8. e (p. 194)
9. a (pp. 194-195)
10. b (p. 195)
11. a (p. 197)
12. e (p. 197)
13. d (p. 199)
14. c (pp. 198-200)
15. b (p. 203)
16. b (p. 201)
17. c (p. 202)

True-False

1. T (p. 189)	7. T (pp. 194-105)	13. T (pp. 197-198)
2. T (p. 196)	8. T (p. 196)	14. T (p. 201)
3. F (p. 193)	9. F (p. 196)	
4. F (p. 194)	10. T (p. 197)	
5. F (p. 196)	11. F (pp. 198-201)	
6. T (pp. 196-197)	12. F (p. 200)	

Experimental Dilemma

1. You should NOT agree with the researchers conclusions. All subjects were tested first at 70, then 90, and then at 40 degree conditions. If you examine the data, you will notice that the subject reaction times improve in the order in which they were tested, thus, these results might be a consequence of carry over effects. Subjects may be improving their reaction time with practice.

2. The experimenter might have controlled for carryover effects by assigning subjects to each condition in a randomized order or by using a counterbalanced order such as a Latin square to assign treatments.

Further Readings

Many psychology students are interested in careers in clinical or counseling psychology. Heppner, Kivlighan, and Wampold (1992) wrote a book focusing on experimental designs and special considerations for research in counseling. You can see how the principles from Chapter 8 are applied to counseling research by reading this book.

Heppner, P., Kivlighan, D. M. Jr., & Wampold, B. E. (1992). *Research design in counseling.* Belmont, CA: Brooks/Cole.

Web Resources

There is an online chapter on *Experimental Design* from *AllPsych Online: The Virtual Psychology Classroom* that may be helpful in understanding the benefits of experimental designs over other research designs. The chapter differentiates between pre-experimental, quasi-experimental, and true experimental designs.
http://allpsych.com/researchmethods/experimentaldesign.html

David Polson, of Athabasca University in Canada, developed a two-part tutorial on internal validity. Part I provides a description of nine threats to internal validity, along with an example and a non-example of each. Part II is an on-line quiz where students must label 36 experiments as internally valid or invalid, and, if invalid, must justify their choice by indicating the relevant threat.
http://psych.athabascau.ca/html/Validity/index.shtml

This site from Geoffrey Urbaniak and S. Plous of Wesleyan University, and sponsored by the Social Psychology Network, provides a highly customizable on-line random number generator that uses JavaScript. You should find the generator useful in assigning participants to conditions and in determining stimulus orders. Tutorials are provided for varied applications.
http://www.randomizer.org/

RESEARCH METHODS WORKSHOPS

The two basic experimental designs are between-subjects and within-subjects designs. Understanding these basic designs facilitates understanding of mixed designs as well as longitudinal and cross-sectional designs. The *Between versus Within Designs* workshop provides additional help for understanding between- and within-subjects designs. Another workshop related to this chapter is *Controls*. Wadsworth's *Research Methods Workshops* can be found at:
http://psychology.wadsworth.com/workshops/.

Chapter 9

Complex Design

Summary
1. Factorial Designs
    1.1. Complex experiments provide
        1.1.1.   increased control
        1.1.2.   greater efficiency
        1.1.3.   greater ecological validity since real world behavior is generally influenced by many factors
    1.2. factorial designs examine all possible combinations of levels of all independent variables
    1.3. a 2x2 experiment in social psychology: the sleeper effect
        1.3.1.   the **sleeper effect** refers to the increased efficacy of a persuasive message with the passage of time
        1.3.2.   a **discounting cue** must be presented with the original message to obtain the sleeper effect
            1.3.2.1. the discounting cue causes one to distrust the persuasive message
        1.3.3.   a 2 x 2 factorial design was used to investigate whether presenting the discounting cue before or after the persuasive message would influence the magnitude of the sleeper effect
            1.3.3.1. one of the independent variables was the *placement* of the discounting cue; the levels were *before* and *after*
            1.3.3.2. the other independent variable was the *delay* between the message and an opinion rating about the topic of the message; the levels were *0 delay* and *6-weeks delay*
            1.3.3.3. Four groups of subjects were tested, one in each combination of these levels; before-0, before-6-weeks, after-0, and after-6-weeks
            1.3.3.4. the **main effect** of placement was found to be small; overall there was a trivial difference between ratings obtained with the before and after discounting cue
            1.3.3.5. The main effect of delay was appreciable; ratings were higher with the 6-week delay than with the 0 delay (this is the sleeper effect)
            1.3.3.6. An **interaction** was found
                1.3.3.6.1.   a much greater sleeper effect was found when the discounting cue was placed after the persuasive message
                1.3.3.6.2.   an interaction occurs when the effects of one independent variable are not the same at different levels of another independent variable
    1.4. patterns of interaction
        1.4.1.   in a factorial experiment, main effects and interactions are entirely independent of each other; any combination of main effects and interactions
107

might occur, and the nature of the interaction is not predictable from knowledge of the main effects

      1.4.2.   A crossover interaction is an important type of interaction

           1.4.2.1. the lines on a graph cross over each other

           1.4.2.2. this kind of interaction cannot be explained by errors in measurement or scaling of the dependent variable

  1.5. control in between-subjects factorial designs

      1.5.1.   the major concern is that *equivalent* groups of subjects are assigned to the various treatment combinations

      1.5.2.   random selection, random assignment, Latin squares, and matching are techniques that are used to try to create equivalent groups

      1.5.3.   a **random-groups design** refers to the unbiased assignment of subjects to groups

      1.5.4.   a matched-groups design in one in which matched sets of subjects are formed and a member from each set is randomly assigned to each treatment combination

2.   Complex Within-Subjects Designs

  2.1. Within-Subject designs provide

      2.1.1.   greater economy than between-subject designs, and

      2.1.2.   guarantee group equivalence

3.   Mixed Designs

  3.1. **mixed designs** have one or more between-subjects independent variables, and one or more within-subjects independent variables

LEARNING THE TERMINOLOGY

Crossover interaction When the effect of one independent variable on a dependent variable reverses at different levels of a second independent variable (p. 219). In a study on the effects of testosterone levels and level of education on male aggression, finding that testosterone increases aggression when education levels are low, but finding the opposite when education level is high, namely, that testosterone decreases aggression when education levels are high.

Discounting cue A message, signal, or pertinent fact that makes you doubt the accuracy or credibility of a persuasive message (p. 212). Finding out that a positive review of a new car was written by the car manufacturer rather than an independent car review magazine.

Interaction Experimental results that occur when the effects of one independent variable depend on the levels of other independent variables (p. 216). In a study on the effects of testosterone levels and level of education on male aggression, finding that the effects of testosterone on aggression are different depending on how much education the male has received.

Main effects When the effect of one independent variable is the same at all levels of another independent variable (p. 214). In a study on the effects of testosterone levels and level of education on male aggression, finding that, regardless of education level, testosterone always increases aggression to some extent; main effect of testosterone.

Matched-groups design Experimental design in which subjects are matched on some variable assumed to be correlated with the dependent variable and then randomly assigned to conditions (p. 221). In a study on the effects of testosterone on male aggression, first testing the aggression of each participant, then matching in pairs those with already high aggression and matching up in pairs those with already low aggressive behavior such that both members of each pair have the same level of aggression. Then randomly assigning each member of each pair to either high or low testosterone administration.

Mixed designs An experimental design that contains both between-subjects and within-subjects manipulations of the independent variable (p. 226). In a study on the effects of testosterone levels and level of education on male aggression, including males with *either* high or low education, but administering *all* participants *both* high and low levels of testosterone.

Part-task simulator A device that simulates only a portion of a system; see *simulator* (p. 226). A computer program operating on a desktop computer that simulates a portion of the cockpit displays of a Boeing 747 rather than simulating the entire experience of flying such a jet.

Random-groups design When subjects are randomly assigned to conditions in a between-subjects design (p. 221). Assigning a number to all the participants in a study and then having a random number generator select the numbers for the participants to be assigned to each treatment.

Simulator A device that duplicates the functions of a real system to allow controlled experiments to be performed (p. 226) A flight simulator that uses motion, computer simulation, and a pretend cockpit to train pilots how to fly airplanes.

Sleeper effect An improvement in the effect of a persuasive message with the passage of time (p. 212). Not believing a positive message about a new car when first reading a review because the review was written by the car manufacturer but still at a later date feeling more positive about the car.

2x2 factorial design A design in which there are two levels of each of two independent variables yielding four conditions (p. 213). In a study on the effects of testosterone levels and level of education on male aggression, having two levels of testosterone (high or low) and two levels of education (some high school vs. university degree).

KEY TERM MATCHING

1.	a. between-subjects factorial design with 2 independent variables, each with two levels
___ 2 x 2 factorial design	
___ matched-group designs	b. has at least one between-subjects and at least one within-subjects independent variable
___ mixed designs	
___ random-groups design	c. sets of similar participants are randomly divided among the treatments
	d. participants are assigned randomly to groups
2.	a. overall differences in the dependent variable among the levels of an independent variable
___ crossover interaction	
___ discounting cue	b. particularly convincing form of an interaction
___ interaction	
___ main effects	c. the effect of one independent variable is not the same at each level of a second independent variable
___ sleeper effect	
	d. information that encourages disbelief of another message
	e. the increase of effectiveness of a persuasive message with the passage of time.

FILL-IN-THE-BLANK

1. Multifactor experiments are likely to have better _____ validity than single-factor experiments.
2. Complex multifactor experiments allow the researcher to make complex causal statements which should increase _____ validity.
3. The phenomenon of an increase in the effectiveness of a persuasive message is called the _____ effect.
4. To obtain a sleeper effect, the persuasive message must be accompanied by a _____ _____.
5. In a 2 x 2 factorial design there are two _____ variables, each with two _____.
6. A factorial experiment includes all possible combinations of all levels of the _____ _____.
7. The effect of a single independent variable is called a _____ effect.
8. An _____ effect occurs when the effects of one independent variable depend upon the level of another independent variable.
9. In an ideal between-subjects experiment, participants would be randomly _____ and then randomly _____ to treatment conditions.

10. In a between-subjects design we want to make sure that the characteristics of the _____ are not confounded with group membership.
11. Two techniques for achieving unbiased assignment of participants to conditions are to _____ assign participants to treatment conditions or to use a balanced _____ _____ to determine group membership.
12. In general researchers try to avoid experimental designs in which potential _____ variables can interact with the independent variable(s).
13. A design in which the assignment of participants to conditions is unbiased is called a _____ - _____ design.
14. In a matched-groups design the _____ are matched on a potentially important variable.
15. A _____-subjects design automatically controls for individual differences.
16. A _____-subjects design requires fewer subjects than does a comparable _____-subjects design.
17. The reduced number of participants tested in a within-subjects design may require that the experimenter increase the number of observations per _____.
18. When there are two independent variables there are _____ possible main effect(s) and _____ possible interaction(s).
19. Whenever an independent variable is manipulated within-subjects there is a possibility of potential _____ effects.
20. _____ designs have one or more between-subjects independent variables and one or more within-subjects variable.

MULTIPLE CHOICE

1. Which of the following is not a reason for doing multifactor experiments instead of several single-factor experiments?
   a. increase the internal validity of the experiments
   b. increase the generality of the results
   c. fewer observations per participant are required in a multifactor experiment
   d. multifactor experiments attempt to match the complexity of forces that combine to influence our thought and behavior
   e. all of the above

2. A factorial experiment
   a. is a between-subjects design.
   b. involves testing all possible combinations of all levels of each independent variable.
   c. allows the researcher to observe interaction effects.
   d. all of the above
   e. both b and c

3. In a 3 x 3 factorial experiment, how many effects can we determine?
   a. 2
   b. 3
   c. 4
   d. 6
   e. 9

4. In a 3 x 2 between-subjects design, there are _____ independent groups and each subject serves in _____ conditions in the experiment.
   a. 5; 1
   b. 5; 2
   c. 6; 1
   d. 6; 2
   e. 6; 6

5. According to the dissociation hypothesis explanation of the sleeper effect,
   a. there is less opinion change over time.
   b. the link between the message and discounting cue strengthens over time.
   c. the message is remembered while the discounting cue is forgotten.
   d. the discounting cue is easier to retrieve.

6. What does it mean when we say that a main effect was obtained in a between-subjects factorial experiment?
   a. The scores obtained under one level of an independent variable were different than the scores obtained under another level of that independent variable.
   b. The mean score from one level of an independent variable was different from the mean score of one level of a different independent variable.
   c. Overall, one independent variable had a larger effect on the dependent variable than did the other independent variables.
   d. The effect of the independent variable was different for different dependent variables.

7. Which of the following describes an interaction effect?
   a. The scores obtained at one level of the independent variable were different than the scores obtained at another level of the independent variable.
   b. The observed effect of one independent variable depends on the level of other independent variables.
   c. The effect of one independent variable was larger for one dependent variable than for another.
   d. The nature of an interaction can only be described when the type of experimental design is known.

8. In a factorial experiment, the number of factors is the number of _____ variables and the number of levels is the number of instances of each _____ variable tested in the experiment.
    a. dependent; dependent
    b. independent; independent
    c. dependent; independent
    d. independent; dependent

9. An interaction effect occurs when
    a. performance in one condition is superior to that in another condition.
    b. performance changes across levels of the independent variable.
    c. the effect of the dependent variable reflects performance in more than one experimental condition.
    d. the effects of one independent variable change depending on the level of another independent variable.

10. An experiment with two factors and two levels of each factor with all possible combinations of these factors is called a _____ factorial.
    a. 2 x 2
    b. 2 x 2 x 2
    c. 2
    d. 2 x 4 x 8

11. Complex multifactor experiments
    a. can be efficient.
    b. can produce results that are difficult to interpret.
    c. allow us to observe both main effects and interaction effects.
    d. all of the above

12. An experiment in which the effects of more than one independent variable are examined simultaneously is called a _____ experiment.
    a. mixed factor
    b. multifactor
    c. single factor
    d. within-subjects

13. When experimental results are presented in a figure, the presence of an interaction is indicated by
    a. positive or negative slope of the lines.
    b. one line that is higher than another.
    c. two (or more) lines that are not parallel to the x-axis.
    d. two (or more) lines that are not parallel to the y-axis.
    e. lines that are not parallel with one another.

14. In a between-subjects factorial design the researcher must make an effort to
    a. ensure that the characteristics of the participant are not confounded with group membership.
    b. equate treatment conditions across the independent groups.
    c. administer all levels of the independent variable to each participant.
    d. control for carry-over effects.

15. The within-subjects design is often used instead of a between-subjects design because
    a. of carry-over effects.
    b. the within-subjects design requires fewer subjects.
    c. the within-subjects design controls for individual differences.
    d. there is not a problem in determining which participants receive the identical treatment orders.
    e. both b and c

16. Compared to a between-subjects random group factorial design, a within-subjects factorial design
    a. requires matching participants on relevant variables.
    b. requires fewer participants.
    c. requires more observations per participant.
    d. all of the above
    e. both b and c

17. A mixed-design experiment is one that contains
    a. an independent variable and a subject variable.
    b. repeated measures and within-subjects factors.
    c. two independent variables that produced an interaction.
    d. at least one between-subject, and at least one within-subject independent variable.

TRUE-FALSE
1. Multifactor experiments are more likely to have ecological validity than single-factor experiments.
2. If possible researchers should start off research in a new area by employing multifactor experiments since these designs are more efficient than single-factor experiments.
3. In a within-subjects design the number of groups of subjects is equal to the product of number of levels of the independent variable times the number of independent variables.
4. In a main effect one dependent variable shows a different pattern of results than the other dependent variable.
5. In order to obtain an interaction at least one of the factors involved in the interaction must have produced a significant main effect.
6. Main effects are more revealing than interaction effects.
7. In a random groups design the experimenter attempts to reduce random variability by equating subjects on variable other than the independent variable(s).

8. Within-subjects designs typically require few observations per subject because each subject serves as their own control.

RESEARCH DILEMMA
Assume you are interested in the effects of caffeine on cognitive processing. You are aware that caffeine tends to improve several aspects of working memory (Warburton, 1996) and decide to determine whether or not caffeine improves performance on a mental rotation task. You design a study similar to the classic mental rotation task used by Shepard and Metzler (1971). You want to make sure your sample is fairly representative so you have an equal number of male and female participants. Half of the participants (10 males and 10 females) receive a placebo 30 minutes prior to completing the mental rotation task. The other half of the participants receives 200 mg of caffeine 30 minutes prior to the mental rotation task. Response time is your dependent variable. Amount of rotation is your independent variable. Results indicate that RT increases with amount of rotation; however, there is no effect of caffeine. You conclude that caffeine does not influence mental rotation. After reading your paper, your professor asks how confident you are in your findings. Should you be concerned about your conclusion?

ANSWERS
KEY TERM MATCHING
1. a, c, b, d
2. b, c, d, a, e

FILL-IN-THE-BLANK
1. ecological (p. 212)
2. ecological (p. 212)
3. sleeper (p. 212)
4. discounting cue (p. 212)
5. independent, levels (p. 213)
6. independent variables (p. 213)
7. main (p. 214)
8. interaction (p. 216)
9. selected, assigned (p. 221)
10. participants (p. 221)
11. randomly, Latin square (p. 221)
12. confounding (pp. 220-221)
13. random-groups (p. 221)
14. participants (p. 221)
15. within (p. 222)
16. within, between (p. 222)
17. participant (p. 222)
18. two, one (p. 214-216)
19. carryover (p. 222)
20. mixed (p. 226)

MULTIPLE CHOICE

1. a (p. 212)
2. e (p. 213)
3. b (p. 213)
4. c (pp. 214-216)
5. c (p. 213)
6. a (p. 214)
7. b (p. 216)
8. b (p. 21-215)
9. d (p. 216)
10. a (p. 213)
11. d (p. 220)
12. b (p. 212)
13. e (p. 219)
14. a (p. 220)
15. e (p. 222)
16. e (p. 222)
17. d (p. 226)

TRUE-FALSE

1. T (p. 212)
2. F (p. 212)
3. F (p. 213)
4. F (p. 214)
5. F (p. 216)
6. F (p. 216)
7. F (p. 221)
8. F (p. 222)

RESEARCH DILEMMA

Your professor is correct. Although you have a well designed study, you are missing an important analysis. Whenever you have more than one independent variable you need to look for interactions. In this case, you need to determine if caffeine interacts with amount of rotation. If there is an interaction it means that response time is influenced by the unique combinations of caffeine and amount of rotation. For example, caffeine may not improve response times for objects rotated 30 deg but may improve response times for objects rotated 120 deg. If there is a significant interaction, it is important to interpret the results in terms of the interaction since main effects may be misleading when interactions exist.

FURTHER READINGS

Neuroimaging has become an important tool in psychological research. However, some critics of this tool suggest that neuroimaging is modern day phrenology and that all neuroimaging tells us is where in the brain a process takes place. Donaldson (2004) argues that neuroimaging can also tell us about what the role of a particular process is when neuroimaging is done in a mixed design. Therefore, this article highlights some of the benefits of conducting mixed design research.

Donaldson, D. I. (2004). Parsing brain activity with fMRI and missed designs: What kind of state is neuroimaging in? *Trends in Neuroscience, 27,* 442-444.

WEB RESOURCES

The Experimental Psychology page of the *Psychology World* website, a site developed by the Department of Psychology and the Instructional Software Development Center at the University of Missouri-Rolla, has several links related to this chapter. These links include information about within-subjects, 2x2 between-subjects, and mixed designs. A slide show on variable selection is also included as is an animation on how confounding can occur through selection. A

printable version of the experimental design module also is provided in pdf (i.e., Adobe Acrobat) format.
http://www.umr.edu/~psyworld/experimental.htm

Bill Trochim's (Cornell University) Web Center for Social Science Research has several Research Methods Tutorials related to this chapter. In particular, under the heading of Research Design & Internal Validity, there are tutorials for Choosing a Research Design, Research Design and Mixed Methods, and Factorial Designs. The website can be found at:
http://www.socialresearchmethods.net/tutorial/tutorial.htm

RESEARCH METHODS WORKSHOPS

True Experiments is a workshop that contains information on multi-factor experiments. The workshop reviews basic features of a true experiment and provides practice in recognizing those features. Single- and multi-factor experiments are contrasted, as are between- and within-subjects designs. A brief review also is included of the use of multiple dependent variables, randomization, and counterbalancing techniques. Wadsworth's *Research Methods Workshops* can be found at:
http://psychology.wadsworth.com/workshops/.

Chapter 10

Small-*n* Experimentation

SUMMARY
1. Small-n Designs
    1.1. the **AB design**
        1.1.1.   baseline condition (A) is followed by a treatment condition (B)
        1.1.2.   used in medical, educational, and other applied research
        1.1.3.   is not recommended because it lacks sufficient control for potential confounding variables
    1.2. the **ABA or Reversal Design**
        1.2.1.   adds a second baseline condition to the AB design to help rule out potential confounds
        1.2.2.   can also use an ABAB design
    1.3. alternating-treatment design
        1.3.1.   more than one independent variable
        1.3.2.   multiple baseline periods
        1.3.3.   example in the text is a study by Rose (1978) who essentially used an ACABCBCB design
    1.4. multiple-baseline design
        1.4.1.   examines the baseline of several behaviors (within the same person) or several different people
        1.4.2.   independent variable is introduced after the baselines
    1.5. changing-criterion design
        1.5.1.   is used for studying the effectiveness of reinforcement often by incrementally increasing the amount of behavior needed to obtain a reward or incrementally decreasing the reward given for a behavior
            1.5.1.1. the independent variable is the criterion
            1.5.1.2. useful for behavioral therapy research
2. Clinical Psychology
    2.1. a case-study on dissociative identity disorder

LEARNING THE TERMINOLOGY
AB design. A frequently used design in therapy in which a therapy (B) is instituted after measuring a particular behavior (A); a poor research design (p. 237). Observing tardiness in an employee, then observing it again once changes have been made to the workplace to reduce tardiness. There are many other things that could have made the employee more punctual than the changes made to the workplace.

ABA design. See reversal (ABA) design

Alternating-treatments design. A small-n design in which two or more independent variables alternate (p. 241). An experiment where an employee's tardiness is measured first for several weeks (baseline) and then two different changes are made to the workplace to improve the employee's morale. First the employee is allowed to play music for 3 weeks, then no music for 3 weeks (baseline) and then later he is allowed instead to have an extra 10 min break once a day for 3 weeks, then back to music for 3 weeks, and then back to getting an extra break for 3 weeks then baseline again. Tardiness is measured each time the level of the independent variable is alternated.

Changing-criterion design. A small-n design in which the criterion behavior needed to produce an outcome changes (p. 246). An experiment assessing the use of a cash bonus to improve a worker's productivity. Rewarding the worker with a bonus for completing 5 projects in a month, then 6 months later only providing the bonus if the workers completes 6 projects/month, then a year later giving the bonus only if the worker completes 8 projects/month.

Functional analysis. An analysis of the antecedents and consequences of a particular behavior; usually undertaken before the implementation of a behavioral treatment (p. 240). A psychologist first observes a child who excessively cries to determine the possible reasons for crying before implementing a therapy to reduce it.

Large-n designs. Designs in which inferential statements are used to determine whether two or more groups differ reliably (p. 235). Having a large number of participants involved in an experiment with proper control groups so that statistics can be used to determine if the treatment is significantly effective.

Multiple-baseline design. A small-n design in which different behaviors or (different participants) receive baseline periods of varying lengths prior to the introduction of the independent variable (p. 242). Observing the amount of crying and fighting in a child and then treating the crying using extinction therapy while monitoring the fighting. Once the crying was reduced, then extinguishing the fighting behavior. Thus, one behavior is allowed to occur under baseline conditions while the other is treated.

Reversal (ABA) design. Small-n design in which a participant's behavior is measured under a baseline (A) condition, then and experimental treatment is applied during the B phase and any changes in behavior are observed; finally, the original baseline (A) conditions are re-instituted to ensure that the experimental treatment was responsible for any observed change during the B phase (p. 237). Observing a patient's depression for a period of time and then introducing an anti-depressant drug therapy. After a length of time, ending the therapy to see if the depression returns during a second baseline.

Small-n design. Research design using a small number of subjects (p. 235). A study by a clinical psychologist to determine if her therapy is effective for a particular patient.

KEY TERM MATCHING

1.	
___ AB design ___ ABA design ___ alternating-treatments design ___ changing-criterion design ___ functional analysis ___ large-*n* design ___ multiple-baseline design ___ small-*n* design	a. a determining the antecedent and consequences of a target behavior b. increasing the amount of a desired behavior necessary for reward c. many observations on a few subjects d. many observations following an extended treatment e. observation of behavior is made before and after a treatment is applied f. small-*n* design that returns to baseline conditions after a treatment has been administered g. small-*n* design used to assess different behaviors or different people h. traditional between- and within-subjects experiments

FILL IN THE BLANK

1. The *n* in a small-*n* design refers to the number of _____.
2. In an AB design, A represents the _____ condition and B represents the condition after the _____ variable had been introduced.
3. Carefully noting the antecedents and consequences of a target behavior prior to using a treatment is called _____ _____.
4. In the AB design the researcher cannot conclusively establish that the variable introduced during the B phase caused the change in behavior, because there is a _____ inherent in this design.
5. Another name for the ABA design is the _____ design.
6. In the ABA design during the second A phase the _____ variable is no longer applied, but the _____ _____ is still recorded.
7. If the behavior during the second A phase of an ABA design, returns to the level of the first A phase, then we can conclude that the _____ variable applied during the _____ phase actually effected the change.

8. In the study by Hart et al. during the B phase the teacher attempted to _____ the crying behavior by not paying attention, while _____ Bill whenever he behaved in an appropriate manner.
9. In the Hart et al, study, the number of crying episodes _____ during the second _____ phase and _____ during both _____ phases.
10. Small-*n* designs often include _____ effects that prohibit the reversal design.
11. A _____ - _____ design might be used to evaluate 2 or more treatments.
12. In Rose's (1978) experiment on the effects of artificial food colors on hyperactivity, the B and C phases include different _____ variables but the same _____ variable is employed in both phases.
13. A _____ - _____ is used when the behavioral requirement for a reward is altered during the course of therapy.
14. Nissen found that faces shown to one personality (would be, would not be) _____ recognized by another personality.
15. Nissen found that words judged as to their pleasantness by one personality, (would be, would not be) _____ used in a word completion task by another personality, at a greater than chance rate.

MULTIPLE CHOICE

1. The *n* in small-*n* designs refers to the number of
   a. dependent variables
   b. independent variables
   c. measurements
   d. participants

2. In small-*n* designs, usually _____ observations are made of _____ participants.
   a. few; few
   b. few; many
   c. many; few
   d. many; many

3. Carefully noting the antecedents and consequences of a target behavior is called _____ _____ and should be done _____ the administration of the treatment.
   a. dysfunctional analysis; before
   b. dysfunctional analysis; after
   c. functional analysis; before
   d. functional analysis; after

4. In an ABA design, A refers to _____ and B refers to _____.
   1. baseline; experimental treatment
   2. baseline; dependent variable
   3. experimental treatment; baseline
   4. experimental treatment; dependent variable

5. When using an AB design in the clinical treatment of maladaptive behavior, the first step is to:
   1. extinguish the maladaptive behavior.
   2. reinforce adaptive behaviors.
   3. obtain a baseline of the maladaptive behavior.
   4. none of the above

6. An AB design is a poor design because
   6. there may be a confounding of uncontrolled factors and level of the independent variable.
   7. it is only appropriate to use with a small-n design.
   8. experimenter bias usually plays a role.
   9. it is impossible to obtain a stable baseline measure with only a single baseline phase.

7. The ABA design
   a. is a large-n design.
   b. is a between-subjects design.
   c. is also called a reversal design.
   d. all of the above

8. Which of the following is considered the more optimum small-n design?
   a. AB designs
   b. ABA designs
   c. ABC designs
   d. ABB designs

9. A common extension of the reversal design that is used when there are more then two treatments, and which provided multiple baseline periods is called
   a. alternating-treatments design.
   b. cumulative-treatments design.
   c. sequential-treatments design.
   d. multiple-baseline design.

10. The multiple-baseline design is useful when
    a. there are permanent carry over effect.
    b. there are several different target behaviors
    c. there are several different people under observation
    d. all of the above

11. If the treatment is likely to have strong carry-over effects, the use of a _____ design is recommended.
    a. alternating-treatments
    b. changing-criterion
    c. multiple-baseline
    d. reversal

12. Rose's study of the effects of oatmeal cookies and artificial food coloring on hyperactivity showed that hyperactivity was highest
    a. with the K-P diet used in the A phase.
    b. with oatmeal cookies, both colored and uncolored.
    c. with artificially colored oatmeal cookies.
    d. with artificially colored K-P diet.

13. Increasing the behavioral requirement that is necessary to earn a reward is an example of the _____ design.
    a. changing-criterion
    b. ABCD
    c. multiple-baseline
    d. partial-reinforcement

14. Nissen, et al. (1988) showed that a patient with a dissociative identity disorder could
    a. easily remember things shown to any of her other personalities.
    b. could only remember things shown to the same personality that was being tested.
    c. had better than chance recognition memory for faces shown to another personality.
    d. had a better than chance probability of using a word shown to another personality in a word completion task.

15. Nissen's study of memory dysfunction in dissociative identity disorders was an example of
    a. an ABA design.
    b. a case study.
    c. operant-conditioning.
    d. time-lag design.

TRUE FALSE
1. Typically in small-n research, a small number of observations are made on many participants.
2. Small-n research is used when Mill's joint method of agreement and difference is not appropriate.
3. The AB design is a very poor small-n design because the researcher cannot be sure the obtained effect is due to the independent variable.

4. The advantage of the ABA design over the AB design is that in the ABA design the second A phase allows the researcher to determine whether the behavior will return to baseline levels when the experimental treatment is no longer applied.
5. In a patient with a dissociative identity disorder, the more ambiguous the memory task, the more likely it is that one personality will have access to information presented to another personality.
6. Alternative-treatments design is appropriate to use when there are permanent carry over effects.
7. The term *functional* in functional analysis refers to the relation between what leads to a specific behavior and the consequences that it produces.
8. The ABAB design is different from ABA because it has an extra baseline period.
9. Large-*n* designs are a better method of research because they focus extensively on the behaviors of individuals.
10. Multiple baseline designs are appropriate for observing several behaviors or several people.

EXPERIMENTAL DILEMMAS

(I)   Imagine that you have a good friend, who is otherwise a fine person, but who has one annoying habit that bothers you. (You can select your friend's bad habit) Moreover, you believe that your friend would be better off socially and be happier, if he/she would only smile more.

   Decide on a 'treatment' that will reduce the frequency of the bad habit, and a second 'treatment' that is likely to increase your friend's smiling behavior. Then figure out a way, using the concepts in this chapter, to determine whether your treatments would be effective.

(II)   Waldo, a mischievous little fellow, liked to play 'hide and seek'. Even when nobody else wanted to play with him he would hide in the strangest places, much to the distress and irritation of his parents. Waldo's Mom, who once had a course in developmental psychology, decided that enough was enough, and spray-painted Waldo a brilliant lilac color, so that he would be easier to find. And Waldo stopped hiding! Mom decided that her 'treatment' had cured Waldo's problem.
Do you agree with Mom?
What kind of a design did she use?
What else might have been responsible for the change in Waldo's behavior?

ANSWER KEY
Key Term Matching
1. e, f, d, b, a, h, g, c

Fill in the Blank
1. participants (p. 235)
2. baseline, independent (p. 237)
3. functional analysis (p. 240)
4. confounding (p. 237)

5. reversal (p. 237)
6. independent, target behavior (p. 237)
7. independent, B (p. 237)
8. extinguish, reward (p. 238)
9. decreased, extinction, increased, baseline (p. 238)
10. carryover (p. 241)
11. alternating-treatments (p. 241)
12. independent, dependent (p. 241)
13. changing criterion (p. 246)
14. would be (p. 248)
15. would not be (p. 248)

Multiple Choice

1. d (p. 235)
2. c (p. 235)
3. c (p. 240)
4. a (p. 237)
5. c (p. 237)
6. a (p. 237)
7. c (p. 237)
8. b (p. 237)

9. a (p. 242)
10. d (p. 243)
11. c (p. 243)
12. c (p. 241)
13. a (p. 246)
14. c (p. 248)
15. b (p. 247)

True False

1. F (p. 235)
2. F (p. 235)
3. T (p. 237)
4. T (p. 237)
5. F (p. 248)

6. F (p. 241)
7. T (p. 240)
8. F (p. 238)
9. F (p. 235)
10. T (p. 243)

Experimental Dilemmas
(I) There are many possible answers to this question. One example might be to use positive reinforcement to remove the bad habit as well as increase smiling. For example, you could pay attention to when your friend is NOT doing the bad habit and comment on nice it was to be around them when they weren't. Then later you could also comment positively every time your friend smiles to encourage more smiling.

One good way to examine the effectiveness of your treatment would be to use a changing-criterion design. First you would monitor their behavior, then later you could make lots of positive comments when your friend was not engaging in the bad habit. Then as the habit decreases, make the positive comments less and less frequently. Do the same for when they smile.

An alternative method would be to use a multiple-baseline design. In this instance, you would monitor both their bad habit and smiling behavior for a baseline period of say 1 week. You would then positively reinforce your friend when he/she was NOT engaging in the bad habit while monitoring his/her smiling baseline. Then, once the bad habit was reduced, you would then start reinforcing smiling behavior.

(II)

You should not agree with Mom. There are potentially numerous reasons why the child stopped hiding other than the spray paint. Such possible confounds make the results of this experiment difficult to interpret.
This was an AB design.
Some examples are that perhaps the child was humiliated by being painted, child hid to get attention and was now getting it, or child grew out of the habit of hiding. Can you think of others?

Further Readings
One of the first psychology researchers, Sigmund Freud, conducted small-*n* research - often on his own daughter! Whether you like his ideas or find them a curiosity, his works are an interesting read on the origins of small-*n* psychology research.

S. Freud, A.A. Brill (Ed.) *The Basic Writings of Sigmund Freud (Psychopathology of Everyday Life, the Interpretation of Dreams, and Three Contributions To the Theory of Sex).* Modern Library, 1995.

S. Freud, J. Strachey (Ed.) *Inhibitions, Symptoms, and Anxieties.* W. W. Norton and Company, 1977.

Long and Clive (1997) provide a brief history of the scientist-practitioner model and the role of small-n design in clinical research.

Long, C. G., & Clive, R. H. (1997). The scientist-practitioner model in clinical psychology: A critique. *Clinical Psychology & Psychotherapy, 4*, 75-83.

Hilliard (1993) describes the essential characteristics of single-case studies and differentiates among three types including single-case experiments, single-case quantitative analysis, and case studies.

Hilliard, R. B. (1993). Single-case methodology in psychotherapy process and outcome research. *Journal of Consulting and Clinical Psychology, 61*, 373-380.

Web Resources

This site was developed from Washington, DC's Center for Effective Collaboration and Practice. The site provides detailed information on how to effectively design and conduct a functional analysis of behavior for problem students.
http://cecp.air.org/fba/default.htm

This site by Paul Jones of the University of Nevada, Las Vegas is entitled *Single-Case Research and Statistical Analysis in School Psychology and Counseling*. It provides a good overview of single-case research designs, including reversal, alternating treatments, and multiple-baseline designs, along with an online quiz. A Java-enabled statistical tool kit also is provided for the evaluation of results from single-case experiments.
http://www.unlv.edu/Colleges/Education/EP/scsaguid.htm#guide0

Chapter 11

Quasi-Experimentation

SUMMARY
1. Internal Validity in Quasi-Experiments
   1.1. **Natural Treatments** are often studied with an *AB* design; behavior before and after some naturally occurring event is compared
       1.1.1.   it is dangerous to attribute behavioral changes to the natural treatment because
           1.1.1.1. the treatment is not under the experimenter's control
           1.1.1.2. most natural treatments have long-term carryover effects
           1.1.1.3. maturation - changes that occur in subjects during the time of the study
           1.1.1.4. history - other changes in the world unrelated to the natural treatment can affect the observed behavior
       1.1.2.   attempts to minimize the effects of maturation and history include adding a nonequivalent control group that is matched to the experimental group ex post facto
           1.1.2.1. this procedure is suspect because of a possible selection bias in forming the control group
   1.2. One-Shot Case Study
       1.2.1.   behavior is observed following a long-term treatment
       1.2.2.   similar to the *AB* design
   1.3. Interrupted-Time-Series Design
       1.3.1.   many observations are made both before and after a naturally occurring treatment
       1.3.2.   marked behavioral changes following the treatment may be due to the treatment, but other interpretations are possible
       1.3.3.   mortality - the loss of subjects over time - is a particular threat to the internal validity of long-term interrupted time series research
       1.3.4.   the internal validity of interrupted-time-series designs can be improved by using an untreated nonequivalent control group or using several dependent variables
   1.4. Designs Employing Subject-Variables
       1.4.1.   **subject-variables** are measurable characteristics of people such as sex, age, attractiveness, etc.
           1.4.1.1. they cannot be manipulated by the experimenter; subjects are *selected* to be in various groups because of these characteristics
       1.4.2.   **matching** subjects on other relevant variables may increase the interval validity of studies employing subject-variables

1.4.2.1. problems with matching include
    1.4.2.1.1.   relevant variables being difficult to measure
    1.4.2.1.2.   important differences may have subtle effects
    1.4.2.1.3.   regression artifacts
1.4.3.   age as a variable
    1.4.3.1. **cross-sectional method** - subjects of various ages are selected to form the experimental groups
        1.4.3.1.1.   age is confounded with generation of birth since people of different ages are born into different social environment
    1.4.3.2. **longitudinal method** - the same subjects are measured at various ages
        1.4.3.2.1.   age is confounded with the state of the world
        1.4.3.2.2.   not only is the subject older, but also the world has changed from one testing to another
    1.4.3.3. **time lag design** - people born in different years are tested when they reach the same age
        1.4.3.3.1.   this procedure allows the time of testing to be evaluated while holding age constant
    1.4.3.4. **cross-sequential design** tests two or more age groups at two or more time periods
        1.4.3.4.1.   this allows the investigator to determine the effects of most of the potential confounds.

LEARNING THE TERMINOLOGY

Cross-sectional method. Taking a large sample of the population of various ages at one time and testing them; *contrast with longitudinal method* (p. 271). A psychologist wishes to know at what age children can learn abstract math. He selects children aged 3, 4, 5, 6, and 7 years and tests their math ability all at the same time.

Cross-sequential design. A quasi-experimental design used when age is a subject variable to try to control for cohort and time of testing effects; involves testing several different age groups at several different time periods; *see longitudinal method and cross-sectional method* (p. 273). A child psychologist testing age when children develop the ability to learn abstract math would test children at various ages at the same time and then again each year as they get older.

History. A possible confound in research that inadvertently takes place between measurements because of historical changes in the participant (p. 255). If testing participants once a week for several weeks to complete an experiment on depression, perhaps the weather may change during the second week and it will rain a lot making some of the participants more depressed and confounding the results.

Interactions. Experimental results that occur when the effects of one independent variable depend on the levels of other independent variables (p.273) The Tversky and Teiffer experiment on age and learning strategies described in the main text on page 271.

Interrupted-time –series design. A quasi-experiment that involves examination of a naturally occurring treatment on the behavior of a large number of participants (p. 260). A researcher examines the rate of vehicle accidents in one area over many years and then after the speed limit has been reduced to determine if accidents decrease.

Longitudinal method. Testing one group of people repeatedly as they age; contrast with cross-sectional method (p. 271). A child psychologist examines when children can learn abstract math by taking a group of children of the same age and testing them each year as they get older.

Matching. A method of control when using subject variables. Subjects are compared with another group with similar characteristics but not the variable of interest (p. 266). A psychologist interested in whether a specific therapy is effective in increasing memory in depressed patients would compare memory performance against other psychiatric patients such as bi-polars or schizophrenics rather than comparing them to healthy participants.

Maturation. Changes in people over time because of growth and other historical factors; may be a source of confounding in quasi-experiments (p. 255). A psychologist studying the effectiveness of one method versus another on teaching children to read would have to be cautious because as time goes on children will be better able to read as they mature independent of teaching method.

Mortality. A possible source of confounding in research resulting from participants dropping out either because they will not participate or because they cannot participate (p. 261). A 10 year study on the effectiveness of ginko biloba to improve memory will have problems with participants dying, moving away or getting tired of the experiment and refusing to continue with it.

Nonequivalent control group. In quasi-experiments a control group that is not determined by random assignment but is usually selected after the fact and is supposed to be equivalent to the naturally treated group (p. 255). A psychologist wishes to test memory during the day versus evening, so he administers memory tests to students in his daytime class and his evening class. Yet, there are probably more differences between students taking day versus evening classes other than the time of day. For example, students attending evening classes are probably older with families or jobs. Thus, they are not an equivalent control group to students attending day classes who are probably younger, full time students.

Observation-treatment-observation. A quasi-experimental design; usually includes a non-equivalent control group (p. 255). Examining the effectiveness of a new method of teaching on reading ability of a third grade class. The experimenter using this design would not be manipulating the variable (teaching method) but merely taking advantage of the fact that the school was.

One-shot case study. A quasi-experiment in which the behavior of a single individual is studied and "explained" in terms of life events (p. 255). see case study and deviant-case analysis.

Quasi-experiment. An experiment in which the independent variable occurs naturally and is not under direct control of the experimenter; *see ex post facto* (p. 255). An experiment on the difference between male and female verbal ability would be quasi experimental because gender is a subject variable, *i.e.* you cannot randomly assign people to be male or female.

Regression artifacts. An artifact in the measurement of change on a variable when groups of subjects who scored at the extremes on the variable are tested again (p. 267). see regression to the mean.

Regression to the mean. Tendency for extreme measures on some variable to be closer to the group mean when re-measured, due to unreliability of measurement (p. 267). If you give a large group of people two IQ tests, in some instances the scores on the first test will be more extreme. Some people will have scored really high on the first test by chance and some will have scored really low because of a bad day. Those really high and really low scoring people will likely score more like everyone else the second time around.

Selection Bias. Occurs when subjects are not selected randomly (p. 255). see non-equivalent control group and matching.

Subject Variable. Some characteristics of people that can be measured or described but cannot be varied experimentally (p. 264). height, weight, sex, or I.Q – see also quasi-experiment.

Synergism. A term used in medical research to describe an interaction; *see interactions* (p. 267). A depressed patient increases by 5 and 6 points respectively on a depression scale when given two different types of antidepressants. However, when given both antidepressants at the same time she scores 20 points higher, suggesting that the antidepressants act synergistically. Thus, the increase in score when taking both is greater than if their effects were merely additive, in which case the score would be 11 points higher.

Time-lag design. A quasi-experimental design used when age is a subject variable in order to control time of testing effects; subjects of a particular age (19 –year-olds) are tested at different time periods (p. 272). A psychologist wishes to test attitudes toward math in 15 year olds. She tests a group of 15 year olds one year, then another groups of 15 year olds the next year and so on.

KEY TERM MATCHING

1.	
___ cross-sectional method ___ cross-sequential design ___ interrupted-time-series design ___ longitudinal method ___ one-shot case study ___ time-lag design	a. AB design for a natural treatment b. compares people born in different years when they reach a specific age c. people born in a particular year are measured at several specific ages d. people born in different years are tested at two or more specific ages e. people of different ages are compared f. several measurements both before and after a natural treatment
2.	
___ history ___ interaction ___ regression artifact ___ maturation ___ mortality ___ quasi-experiment	a. changes in subjects over time that confound the interpretation of a natural treatment b. distortion resulting from statistical regression to the mean c. experiments that include one or more uncontrolled variables d. possible problem associated with matching e. the effect of one independent variable depends of the level of a second independent variable f. uncontrolled changes in a setting that confound the interpretation of a natural treatment

3.	
___ subject variable	a. attempt to form a comparison group in quasi-experiments
___ synergism	b. comparison subjects that are matched to subjects who have been exposed to a natural treatment
___ nonequivalent control group	c. measurable characteristic on which people differ
___ matching	d. interaction in which the combined effects of two variables exceed the sum of their individual effects

FILL IN THE BLANK

1. Quasi-experiments allow the researcher to examine variables that would be _____ to manipulate directly.

2. Most quasi-experiments involving naturally occurring events are similar in structure to small-n _____ designs.

3. Quasi-experiments of the general form observation-treatment-observation are not true reversal designs because
(a)_____
_____ and
(b)_____
_____

4. Two threats to internal validity with naturally occurring treatments are the _____ of the participant and any changes in the _____ that occur over time.

5. In a nonequivalent control group design the experimenter attempts to _____ two groups after one group has received some treatments.

6. The primary threat to internal validity associated with the one-shot case study is the lack of a _____ _____.

7. In a typical case study the researcher gains control by increasing the _____ of observations.

8. In long-term time series studies the participants may be unavailable late in the study, a confounding factor that is called _____. This confounding would lead to a special form of _____ bias.

9. The difficulties of the interrupted-time-series design are magnified when the _____ of the treatment is delayed or masked by other variables.

10. Sex, height, and IQ are all _____ variables.

11. Designs employing subject variables essentially produce _____ between variables.
12. A problem inherent in studies employing subject variables is that whatever results are obtained may be caused by _____ variables.
13. One way to avoid confounding with subject variables is _____.
14. Matching often greatly reduces _____ size.
15. Synergism of two variables means that the two variables do not have _____ effects but rather they _____.
16. Matching may lead to _____ artifacts.
17. In a _____ design the same participant is tested repeatedly over a long time period.
18. In a _____-_____ design the researcher selects children from different ages and observes their behavior on one occasion.
19. Age is not a true _____ variable.
20. As an individual goes through life he maintains the same _____, or group of people born at approximately the same time period.
21. A time-lag design attempts to determine the effects of the time of _____ while holding _____ constant.

MULTIPLE CHOICE

1.   Quasi-experiments in the general form observation-treatment-observation cannot be true reversal designs because
   a. most natural treatments have long-term carry-over effects.
   b. there is no control condition.
   c. the variables are generally confounded.
   d. all of the above

2.   One way to obtain a "control" group or condition in case-study research is to
   a. employ a time-series design.
   b. employ a deviant-case analysis.
   c. replicate the research in a controlled laboratory experiment.
   d. randomly assign subjects to either the case-study condition or the control condition.

3.   In a time-series analysis we are interested in
   a. consistent patterns of responding across the individuals' life span.
   b. separating changes in behavior that are due to maturation from changes that are due to treatment effects.
   c. determining the relative effect of a treatment as a function of when the treatment was introduced.
   d. changes following introduction of the treatment.

4. One way to increase internal validity in case study research is to use
    a. deviant case analysis.
    b. nonequivalent control groups.
    c. multiple dependent variables.
    d. all of the above

5. Which of the following is not a subject variable?
    a. sex of individual
    b. political affiliation
    c. weight
    d. age
    e. all of the above are subject variables

6. Which of the following represents a quasi-experimental research project?
    a. Memory performance is compared between a group of subjects who study material for 10 minutes versus a group who studies for 20 minutes.
    b. Perception of light flashes is compared between subjects who are dark-adapted and those who are not.
    c. SAT scores are compared for students in private and public schools.
    d. Arousal level is measured as a function of type of music presented to subjects.

7. Which of the following is true concerning quasi-experimental designs?
    a. they are less powerful than observational studies
    b. they often include subject variables
    c. they involve careful manipulation of experimental variables
    d. they are rarely used in psychological research

8. Matching
    a. is used in quasi-experiments.
    b. is a way of avoiding confounding of subject variables.
    c. introduces the possibility of regression artifacts.
    d. all of the above

9. If a researcher wants to use a research design that employs subject variables, then that researcher will
    a. manipulate the subject variable holding other factors constant.
    b. select subjects who have the chosen characteristics in some varying degree.
    c. select a behavior to measure that will not vary with the subject variable.
    d. none of the above.

10. In designs that employ subject variables, matching refers to
    a. matching subjects on the subject variables.
    b. matching subjects on the behavioral task that is measured.
    c. matching subjects on the variables that may be confounded with the subject variable.
    d. matching subjects on variables that are known to be confounded with the behavioral task.

11. The phenomenon of regression to the mean implies that if two abnormally tall parents have a child, the child's adult height will likely be
    a. shorter than the mean of the parents' heights.
    b. taller than the mean of the parents' heights.
    c. close to the mean of the parents' heights.
    d. exactly between the parents' heights.

12. A synergistic relationship among two variables indicates that
    a. the two variables interact.
    b. the two variables are correlated.
    c. the two variables are confounded.
    d. The two variables are additive.

13. Given that age is a subject variable,
    a. it may be directly manipulated in an experimental design.
    b. it is easy to attribute causation to the age factor as opposed to any other factor in an experimental design.
    c. it is examined largely in correlational studies rather than in experimental designs.
    d. it may only be treated as a control variable in developmental research.

14. A researcher interested in the long-term effects of nuclear wastes monitors the health of 15 families living near a waste disposal site. The researcher records any instance of physical or mental illness reported by the families over a period of 10 years. This sort of study is called a _____ design.
    a. cross-sectional
    b. cross-sequential
    c. longitudinal
    d. time-lag

15.   In a longitudinal design
       a.   the confoundings inherent in cross-sectional designs are avoided.
       b.   results may be produced by historical events occurring during the course of
            the study.
       c.   the same group of subjects are repeatedly tested as they grow older.
       d.   all of the above

16.   Cross-sectional research designs
       a.   allow for causal inferences concerning the effects of subject variables.
       b.   confound age with other subject variables of interest.
       c.   are much more difficult to run than longitudinal studies.
       d.   all of the above

TRUE FALSE
1.   Ex post facto analysis involving more than one dependent variable may be
      interpreted in a causal fashion.
2.   Quasi-experiments of the general form observation-treatment-observation can best
      be considered a reversal, or ABA design.
3.   Two threats to internal validity with naturally occurring treatments are the history
      of the subject and changes in the subject that occur over time.
4.   In a nonequivalent control group, matching is attempted after the occurrence of the
      treatment.
5.   An interrupted-time-series design is the best design that can be used when the size
      of the effect of the treatment is expected to be delayed for some period.
6.   Ability to recall dreams is an example of a subject variable.
7.   When manipulating a subject variable it is important to hold all other factors
      constant.
8.   Studies involving subject variables essentially produce correlations between
      variables.
9.   Matching subjects on relevant variables avoids problems caused by confounding.
10.   Regression procedures often lead to matching artifacts.
11.   In a synergistic relationship the two variables exhibit additive effects.
12.   Matching often reduces the size of the sample on which observations are made.
13.   Matched variables are rarely under direct control.
14.   Regression to the mean refers to the phenomenon whereby if people who receive
      extreme scores on some characteristic are retested, their second scores tend to be
      closer to the group mean than were their first scores.
15.   In a cross-sectional research design, the same subjects are repeatedly tested over
      the course of several years.
16.   Longitudinal and cross-sectional studies can produce different results due to the
      fact that age may be confounded with other factors in cross-sectional designs.

17. The confounding inherent in cross-sequential designs is eliminated in longitudinal studies.
18. Longitudinal designs tend to confound age with other subject variables.
19. Time-lag designs determine the effects of time of testing while holding age constant.
20. Cross-sequential designs include both longitudinal and cross-sequential components.

EXPERIMENTAL DILEMMAS

(I)   As part of an investigation of the effects of biorhythms on various physical and psychological abilities a researcher decided to measure absolute threshold early in the morning and then again late at night. Each morning the researcher went to his laboratory at 6:00 a.m. and tested his participants' absolute threshold, using the method of limits to determine the absolute threshold for detecting a 400 Hz tone embedded in white noise. At night the participants reported to the University Sleep Lab to be tested. The Sleep Lab was equipped with a microcomputer, which makes it easy to test the participants' absolute threshold using the staircase method. As in the morning session, the participants' task was to detect the presence of a 400 Hz tone embedded in white noise.

The results showed that, on average, the participants' absolute threshold was lower in the morning than in the evening. That is, the absolute threshold stimulus intensity was lower in the morning than in the evening. The researcher concluded that time of day has an effect upon auditory absolute threshold, with people being more sensitive in the morning than in the afternoon.

Do you agree or disagree with this conclusion? Why or why not?

(II)   A psychologist interested in the effect of personality traits upon various psychological abilities decided to test whether introverts or extroverts are more sensitive to external stimulation. His hypothesis was that introverts, who are basically quiet, shy people, would be more sensitive to the external world than would extroverts, who he thought would be more sensitive to internal stimulation. To test this hypothesis he decided to see which group of subjects would be better able to detect a very faint amount of pressure applied to the back of the hand.

Ten introverts and 10 extroverts were selected on the basis of a personality test. All participants were paid for taking part in the study. Participants were each tested individually by the same experimenter. Participants were blindfolded and then given 200 trials. On half of the trials, a very faint amount of pressure was applied to the back of the participant's hand by means of a mechanical device. The amount of pressure was constant for all participants. On the remaining trials no pressure was applied to the participants hand. All participants were right handed, and only the right hand was used in the experiment. Finally, a different random order of pressure trials and no pressure trials was used for each participant. Participants were not told how many trials there would be, only that there would be "a lot." No participant was told what percentage of trials would be "touch" trials.

Results showed that, averaged across participant, the extroverts responded correctly on 85% of the touch trials and were incorrect on 15% of these trials. Introverts, however were only correct on 70% of the touch trials, making 30% errors on these trials. These differences between groups were reliable.

The research concluded that these results indicated that extroverts were more sensitive than introverts, since they were correct on more of the touch trials (85% versus 70%). Since this was exactly the opposite of what he had predicted he decided that his hypothesis needed to be revised.

Do you agree with this conclusion? Why or why not? How would you design an experiment to test this hypothesis?

(III) A researcher submitted the following work to a journal for publication. Twenty second-graders were selected to participate in a remedial reading program based on scores obtained on a general reading skills test given to all children in the school system. The students were chosen because they did not perform as well as their classmates in general reading skills, and it was hoped that the program would improve their reading ability. The program involved individual sessions with a special instructor three hours a week for six weeks. At the end of this period, the test was re-administered to the students in the program. Scores were compared with those of children of similar ability from another grammar school in the area who took the test again at the same point in the school year as the children in the remedial program. The results showed no difference between scores for students who had participated in the remedial program and those who had not. Although the researcher wanted to conclude that the program had been ineffective, a reviewer argued that the results could have been due to regression artifacts. Do you agree with the reviewer? Why or why not?

(IV) Using the same example as in chapter 9, assume you are interested in the effects of caffeine on cognitive processing. You are aware that caffeine tends to improve several aspects of working memory (Warburton, 1996) and decide to determine whether or not caffeine improves performance on a mental rotation task. You design a study similar to the classic mental rotation task used by Shepard and Metzler (1971). You want to make sure your sample is fairly representative so you have an equal number of male and female participants. Half of the participants (10 males and 10 females) receive a placebo 30 minutes prior to completing the mental rotation task. The other half of the participants receives 200 mg of caffeine 30 minutes prior to the mental rotation task. Response time is your dependent variable. Amount of rotation is your independent variable. Results indicate that RT increases with amount of rotation; however, there is no effect of caffeine. This time you look at the interaction between caffeine and rotation and find no interaction. You again conclude that caffeine does not influence mental rotation. After reading your paper, your professor asks you if you are still confident in your findings. Should you still be concerned about your conclusion?

ANSWER KEY
Key Term Matching
1. e, d, f, c, a, b
2. f, e, b, a, d, c
3. c, ,d b, a

Fill in the Blank
1.   unethical (p. 254)
2.   experimental (p. 254)
3.   a) treatment is not under experimenter's control, b) treatment likely to have carryover effects (p.254)
4.   maturation, setting (p.254)
5.   match (p.255)
6.   control condition (p.256)
7.   number (p.256)
8.   mortality, selection (p.261)
9.   effect (p.261)
10. subject (p.264)
11. correlations (p.266)
12. confounding (p.266)
13. matching (p.266)
14. sample (p.267)
15. additive, interact (p.267)
16. regression (p.267)
17. longitudinal (p.271)
18. cross-sectional (p.271)
19. independent; (p.271)
20. cohorts (p.272)
21. testing, age (p.272)

Multiple Choice

1. d (p. 254)	9. b (p. 264)
2. b (p. 256)	10. c (p. 266)
3. c (p. 260)	11. a (p. 267)
4. d (p. 264)	12. a (p. 267)
5. e (p. 264)	13. c (p. 271)
6. c (p. 269)	14. c (p. 271)
7. b (p. 264)	15. d (p. 271)
8. d (p. 266)	16. b (p. 273)

True False

1. F (p. 254)	11. F (p. 267)
2. F (p. 254)	12. T (p. 267)
3. T (p. 255)	13. T (p. 267)
4. T (p. 255)	14. T (p. 267)
5. T (p. 260)	15. F (p. 271)
6. T (p. 264)	16. T (p. 271)
7. F (p. 265)	17. F (p. 272)
8. T (p. 265)	18. F (p. 271)
9. F (p. 266)	19. T (p. 272)
10. F (p. 267)	20. T (p. 273)

Experimental Dilemmas

(I) You should disagree with the conclusions. The experimenter used a different method for assessing absolute threshold for the morning and late night tests. Thus, two times cannot really be compared. Secondly, the experiment could be confounded with maturation effects. By testing them all in the morning first, then all at night second, something could have happened during the day to change the way participants responded.

(II) There may be a confounding variable in this experiment. Different personality types (introvert vs. extrovert) may have different rates of responding. That is, one may be more confident in their judgment of whether they may have felt the pressure than another producing more false positive and correct positive responses. This experiment should be conducted again at to test whether response rates are different in the two groups.

(III) You may wish to agree with the reviewer. According to the main text (p. 227-228), regression artifact is a serious problem when matching is used in research. In this instance, because the students from two different schools were matched (rather than randomly assigned), we cannot rule out the idea that the results may be a consequence of regression toward the mean.

(IV)   Your professor is still correct. Once again, you have a well-designed study but are missing an important analysis. Most of the time researchers treat individual differences as sources of error. In this case, however, sex differences are known to exist on mental rotation tasks. Furthermore, there is some recent evidence suggesting that caffeine may affect men and women differently. Therefore, you should include sex as a subject variable in your analysis to determine if (1) there is a sex difference on the mental rotation task and (2) an interaction between sex and caffeine conditions. If there is an interaction, the effects of caffeine are influenced by whether or not the participant is a male or female. Thus, your conclusion would change.

FURTHER READINGS
For those interested in child development, Scott Miller has written a very good book on research methods in this area.

Miller, S. A. (1998). *Developmental Research Methods*. New Jersey: Prentice Hall.

If you are interested in clinical psychology, you may want to refer to:

Roberts, M. C., & Ilardi, S. S. (Eds.). (2003). *Handbook of research methods in clinical psychology*. Malden, MA: Blackwell.

Another interesting resource is a book by Shadish, Cook, and Campbell (2002). The authors address the ability to make causal inferences with experimental and quasi-experimental designs.

Shadish, W. R., Cook, T. D., & Campbell, D. T. (2002) *Experimental and quasi-experimental designs for generalized causal inference*. Boston, MA: Houghton Mifflin.

WEB RESOURCES
This section of Bill Trochim's (Cornell University) Research Methods Knowledge Base presents several quasi-experimental designs and discusses their implementation and limits. Primary points include the use of nonequivalent control groups and regression to the mean. Links are provided to other types of quasi-experiments, including descriptions of various pre-post-test designs. There is also a link to an online reprint from the site's author on advances in quasi-experimentation.
http://www.socialresearchmethods.net/kb/quasiexp.htm

RESEARCH METHODS WORKSHOPS

The *Nonexperimental Approaches* workshop tutorial describes various types of nonexperimental designs while focusing on the advantages and disadvantages of each designs. In addition, the tutorial provides examples of the types of data you would examine for each design. Wadsworth's *Research Methods Workshops* can be found at: http://psychology.wadsworth.com/workshops/.

Chapter 12

Conducting Ethical Research

SUMMARY
1. Research with Human Participants
   1.1. responsible psychologists follow the ethical guidelines provided by the American Psychological Association, including
      1.1.1. obtaining institutional approval to conduct research (the approved protocol must be followed)
      1.1.2. obtaining informed consent from each participant
      1.1.3. required informed consent for recording voices or images
      1.1.4. subordinates to the research should be allowed to withdraw or decline participation without penalty; students should have an alternative assignment available if class credit is given for research participation
      1.1.5. informed consent is not necessary when the research is conducted in benign setting, there is little chance of harm, confidentiality and anonymity are ensured, and no legal liability is associated with the study
      1.1.6. excessive incentives for participation may be seen as coercive and should be avoided
      1.1.7. deception should not be used unless deception is required to obtain unbiased data and nondeceptive alternatives are not available
      1.1.8. debriefing participants so that they are informed about the research and negative consequences are corrected retaining the responsibility for ensuring ethical practices
      1.1.9. proper care and use of animals in research
   1.2. informed consent and deception
      1.2.1. participants are told before the study all factors that might reasonably be expected to influence their willingness to participate
         1.2.1.1. participants rarely misled
         1.2.1.2. usually state the purpose of the study truthfully
            1.2.1.2.1. sometimes deception is used (e.g., false description or cover story) to control participant reactivity – misleading information
            1.2.1.2.2. deception is used less frequently regarding the purpose of an experiment (e.g., not letting the participants know the study is a memory experiment) – information withheld
            1.2.1.2.3. then benefits of the research involving deception must outweigh the actual and potential costs to the participants
   1.3. Freedom to Withdraw
      1.3.1. participants have the right to withdraw from the study

      1.3.2.   when potential coercion exists (e.g., participating in a study because it is a class requirement), participants need to be able to withdraw from the study

           1.3.2.1.   alternative activities should be available when research participation is a class requirement

           1.3.2.2.   research done for extra credit is more voluntary

1.4. Protection from Harm and Debriefing

      1.4.1.   **protection from harm** – participants should be able to receive help or advice after the research is completed if problems arise from participation

      1.4.2.   **debriefing** includes a description of the experimental manipulations and an opportunity to answer any questions about the study or to clarify any misunderstandings about the study

1.5. Removing Harmful Consequences

      1.5.1.   the researcher has the responsibility to **remove harmful consequences** so that participants do not suffer long-term consequences for their participation

      1.5.2.   participants should feel the same after the study as they did before the study

1.6. Confidentiality

      1.6.1.   what a participants does and what information a participants provides during the course of a study should be confidential unless there is an agreement with the participant

      1.6.2.   confidentiality should be maintained unless it is necessary to break confidentiality in order to protect a participants from harm

2.   Ethics in Research with Animals

2.1. animals are used in research because

      2.1.1.   it would be difficult or impractical to answer certain questions with human participants

      2.1.2.   animals are interesting in their own right

      2.1.3.   animals provide convenient, highly controlled models for humans and for other animals

2.2. arguments against research with Animals

      2.2.1.   animals feel pain and their lives can be destroyed, as is true of humans

      2.2.2.   destroying any living thing is dehumanizing to the scientist

      2.2.3.   using animals in research is a form of prejudice called speciesism and as such, is completely unethical

2.3. arguments for research with animals

      2.3.1.   guidelines and ethical standards for animal research guard against undue pain and the inhumane treatment of animals

           2.3.1.1. much of the research on animals does not involve pain

      2.3.2.   if the destruction of any living thing is dehumanizing then we should not benefit from the destruction of animals in any way including animals as a source of food, products (e.g., leather), or medical advances

           2.3.2.1. such a position is often difficult to maintain

2.3.2.2. a survey of animal rights activists showed that the majority (53%) eat meat and/or purchase leather goods
  2.3.3.   in regard to scientific progress at the expense of animals being speciesism
    2.3.3.1. much animal research benefits other animals
    2.3.3.2. few people would be willing to give up the benefits that derive from animal research including advances in neurosurgery and understanding and treatment of many psychological disorders
2.4. guidelines for use of animals in research include
  2.4.1.   acquisition, care, use, and disposal of all animals in compliance with the law
  2.4.2.   supervision by a trained psychologist of all procedures involving animals
  2.4.3.   minimizing pain, discomfort, and illness of animals
  2.4.4.   terminating an animal's life rapidly and painlessly
3. Scientific Fraud
  3.1. cases of deliberate research bias include
    3.1.1.   Sir Cyril Burt's work on heredity and intelligence
    3.1.2.   the Piltdown Man
    3.1.3.   fraud will eventually be discovered through the self-correcting nature of the scientific method and direct **replications** of research
  3.2. **plagiarism** is taking credit for someone else's ideas, data, or words
4. Monitoring Ethical Practices
  4.1. the American Psychological Association established an Ethics Committee which
    4.1.1.   educates the public and psychologists
    4.1.2.   investigates complaints about unethical research practices
  4.2. the **Institutional Review Boards (IRB)**
    4.2.1.   required by institutions receiving federal funds for research
    4.2.2.   approve proposed research at these institutions

LEARNING THE TERMINOLOGY

Confidentiality Information obtained about subjects should remain confidential unless otherwise agreed upon (p. 285)

Debriefing When subjects are told all details of an experiment after they have participated; an ethical obligation of the researcher (p. 284)

Deception A research technique in which the participant is misled about some aspect of the project; may be unethical (p. 282)

Fraud Deliberate bias, in the research process, that includes fabrication of data and plagiarism (p. 299)

Freedom to withdraw Experimenter is ethically obligated to allow subjects to discontinue participation in the research (p. 283)

Informed Consent Potential subjects must be in a position to decide whether to participate in an experiment (p. 282)

Institutional Review Board A board in nearly every US institution conducting research that oversees the protection of human participants (p. 294)

Plagiarism The uncredited use of another person's words or ideas (p. 293)

Protection from harm Ethical researchers protect their participants from any harm (p. 284)

Removing harmful consequences Ethical researchers remove any harmful consequences that their participants may have incurred (p. 285)

Replication The repetition of an earlier experiment to duplicate its findings). An important technique to reveal fraudulent data (p. 293)

Speciesism A term used to describe the view that animal life is qualitatively different from human life and, therefore, a form of bigotry (p. 288)

KEY TERM MATCHING

1.		
___ aftercare	a.	a committee that monitors ethical practices at an institution
___ confidentiality	b.	allowing a participant to call a halt to his continued participation in an experiment
___ debriefing		
___ deception	c.	deliberate misrepresentation of research results
___ fraud		
	d.	ensuring that a participant is in as good physical and mental shape at the end of an experiment as he is at the beginning
___ freedom to withdraw		
___ informed consent		
___ institutional review board	e.	explaining to a participant the purpose of an
___ protection from harm		experiment at its

		conclusion
___ removing harmful consequences	f.	given by the participant before participation in a study
___ replication	g.	a manipulation to reduce reactivity
___ speciesism	h.	not talking about the experimental performance of individual participants
	i.	prejudice against lower animals
	j.	process by which science is self-correcting
	k.	responsibility for possibly long-term effects
	l.	the overriding ethical principle

FILL-IN-THE-BLANK

1. Most universities and research institutions have _____ committees that judge the ethicality of proposed research.
2. Individuals should read and understand the ethical principles of the American Psychological Association _____ they conduct a research project with human participants.
3. Participants should be warned ahead of time if there are any potential _____ _____ that might result from participating in the experiment.
4. The experimenter is obliged to _____ participants of any potential harm. .
5. Psychologists who conduct research with human participants are obliged to respect the _____ and _____ of the participants in the research.
6. Individuals must be given the option of _____ from the research at any time.
7. Deception is sometimes used to control participant _____.
8. When students taking an introductory psychology course are required to participate in experiments as part of a course requirement, they should have some _____ way of fulfilling this requirement.
9. _____ means that the experimenter explains the general purposes of the research and the nature of the manipulations used.
10. Unless otherwise agreed, what a subject does in an experiment should be _____.
11. Ethical decisions are rarely made on the basis of _____ facts.
12. _____ is a form of racism involving claims about scientific progress being helped by animal research.

148

13. Animal subjects should be treated humanely, and the decision to inflict pain on an animal should be based on a weighing of the _____ and _____ of the research.
14. As a model for _____ and _____ behavior, animal research is essential for scientific progress.
15. _____ is intentional researcher bias. It can be detected when other researchers fail to _____ the original results.

MULTIPLE CHOICE

1. The principle of informed consent means that the researcher has an obligation to
   a. submit all research proposals to a peer committee that will judge the ethics of the proposed research.
   b. tell subjects prior to participation all aspects of the research that might reasonably be expected to influence willingness to participate.
   c. only disclose the results of the experiment after he has obtained the consent of all subjects who participated in the study.
   d. agree to perform the research only after he or she is certain that no ethical standards are being violated.

2. According to the current APA ethical guidelines, which statement below about informed consent is true?
   a. If video recordings are acquired without a participant's awareness, informed consent can be obtained after the fact.
   b. Participants do not always need to be told about possible risks in advance of their participation.
   c. Researchers always have to obtain informed consent.
   d. Participants do not need to be know if deception was used in the study.

3. In an ethical research project
   a. informed consent is obtained from all participants.
   b. participants may withdraw at any time.
   c. the potential gains outweigh the potential harm.
   d. all of the above
   e. both a and b

4. In the Elmes, et al study on depression and memory
   a. the researchers did not deceive the participants.
   b. both the experimental and control group received depression induction.
   c. subjects in the control group responded as if they were depressed.
   d. participants were given a list of people to contact if the depression continued.

5. One problem associated with providing enough information for informed consent is that
   a. the validity of the experimental design may be undermined.
   b. people may avoid participating in all psychology research, even low-risk studies.
   c. some research projects may not be able to obtain subjects.
   d. it is a time-consuming process.

6. Debriefing means that
   a. the investigator is aware of the potential risks involved is the experiment.
   b. the investigator explains the general purpose of the research after the study is completed.
   c. the investigator provides the ethics committee with an abstract of each proposed research project.
   d. after a blind experiment is run the investigator tells the research assistants what the purpose of the experiment was.

7. Experiments involving deception
   a. should be avoided because participants feel devalued once they learn of deception during debriefing.
   b. probably should not be done on ethical grounds.
   c. are acceptable in animal research.
   d. obligates the researcher to explain the true nature of the experiment after the participant has been tested.

8. A participant can choose to withdraw from a study
   a. only during the informed consent phase
   b. for any reason at any point during the study
   c. but will not receive any compensation (e.g., class credit)
   d. after the experimenter explains the adverse effect withdrawing from the study would have on the data collection process

9. An experiment that is potentially harmful to human participants
   a. is still acceptable as long as the potential harm is clearly outlined during informed consent
   b. is permissible as long as a physician or paramedic is at the study site
   c. is appropriate if the participants have thrill-seeking personalities
   d. should be pursued by nonexperimental methods

10. Research with animals is similar to that with humans because
    a. the researcher must still obtain informed consent
    b. approval must be obtained through the appropriate IRB
    c. debriefing is needed to maintain the animal's sense of well-being
    d. animals frequently need to be deceived to respond naturally

11. Animal researchers need to
    a. anthropomorphize.
    b. engage in speciesism.
    c. provide evolutionary-based interpretations.
    d. treat animals humanely.

12. Animals are often used as subjects in psychological research because
    a. ethical considerations are generally less stringent with animal research than with human research.
    b. they are interesting.
    c. they form an important part of the natural world.
    d. all of the above
    e. both b and c

13. Singer (1978) calls claims about scientific progress being helped by animal research
    a. anthropomorphism.
    b. explicitly unethical.
    c. speciesism.
    d. unfounded.
    e. all of the above

14. Which of these people/groups are NOT involved in discovering fraud?
    a. ethical review boards
    b. individual researchers
    c. federal granting agencies
    d. Piltdown foundation

15. Minimal risk refers to
    a. research that has no greater risk than that associated with everyday life
    b. the least amount of risk associated with a given research design
    c. research in which no deception is used
    d. situations in which adequate medical or psychological help is provided after the study

TRUE-FALSE

1. Any federally funded research must be approved by an ethics review committee before any funding is granted.
2. In a research project, every member of the research team is responsible for ensuring ethical practice in research.
3. In the Elmes, et al (1984) study on the effect of depression on memory, subjects were told about the possible side effects of the depressant drug during the debriefing session.
4. Providing information for informed consent generally helps reduce the reactivity of the experimental design.
5. Participants are always allowed to withdraw from an experiment regardless of their reasons for withdrawing.
6. Informed consent is generally obtained in writing during the debriefing session.
7. Confidentiality means that, in general, results of an experiment are not published unless the subject gives his or her approval.
8. Ethical decisions are never made on the basis of pragmatic concerns.

EXPERIMENTAL PROJECT

This project is designed to get you to consider in more detail the issues of ethics in research. Make up a short list of experiments that you think are in some way unethical, but that you might like to perform just to see what happens. Visit faculty members who specialize in the research areas of your experiments and ask them if they would be willing to supervise the experiments.

Did the faculty members question the ethics of your proposed experiment? How many faculty members told you that they refuse because the proposed research is unethical? How many tried to see if there might be a way to answer the question posed in your research, but using an ethical experiment? Finally, after reading the issues raised in the chapter, would you consider this to be an ethical project? Why or why not?

EXPERIMENTAL DILEMMA

You are interested in using an Asch-type experiment to examine how people's perceptions of acceptable displays of affections can be influenced by others. After you design the study and have it approved by the IRB, you consult your confederates to see when they have available times to do the study. You post a sign-up sheet for "Sex Research" on a bulletin board in the department so that students can sign up to participate in the study at a designated time. However, before you are able to conduct the study, the department chair requests to see you. Do you have any idea why?

ANSWERS
Key Term Matching

1. k, h, e, g, c, b, f, a, l, d, j, i

Fill-in-the-blank
1. peer (p. 279)
2. before (p. 280)
3. detrimental effects (p. 282)
4. inform (p. 282)
5. dignity, welfare (p. 281)
6. withdrawing (p. 283)
7. reactivity (p. 282)
8. optional (p. 283)
9. debriefing (p. 284)
10. confidential (p. 284)
11. objective (p. 286)
12. speciesism (p. 288)
13. costs, benefits (p. 289)
14. human, animal (p. 291)
15. fraud, replicate (p. 292)

Multiple Choice
1. b (p. 282)
2. a (p. 280)
3. d (p. 284)
4. d (p. 282)
5. a (p. 282)
6. b (p. 282)
7. d (pp. 281-282)
8. b (pp. 283-284)
9. d (p. 289)
10. b (p. 289)
11. d (pp. 290-291)
12. d (p. 288)
13. c (p. 288)
14. d (p. 293)
15. a (p. 295)

True-False
1. T (p. 294)
2. T (p. 281)
3. F (p. 285)
4. F (p. 283)
5. T (p. 283)
6. F (p. 282)
7. F (p. 285)
8. F (p. 286)

RESEARCH DILEMMA
Although you have gone through the appropriate channels by receiving IRB approval to conduct the study, your sign-up process did not protect your participants. Anyone walking down the hall could stop at the bulletin board and see all the names of people who signed-up for sex research. Unfortunately, that information could be abused by others. Whenever you are conducting research on sensitive matters, it is good to maintain anonymity as well as confidentiality.

FURTHER READINGS
Association for the Study of Animal Behavior, & Animal Behavior Society (Ethical and Animal Care Committees). (2002). *Animal Behavior, 63*(1), 195-199.

This article from two major animal research organizations provides ethical guidelines that go beyond existing APA principles and that should aid cost-benefit analyses of research. Included are alternatives to animal research, species considerations, and legislation issues, as well as new recommendations for acquisition, care, and disposal.

Sales, B. D., & Folkman, S., (Eds.). (2000). *Ethics in research with human participants*. Washington, DC: American Psychological Association.
This text is an updated form of the commonly used APA book *Ethical Principles in the Conduct of Research with Human Participants*, and represents a powerful resource to current and future researchers. It summarizes the response of a 1994 APA task force to recent changes not only in research contexts, but also normative views on ethical issues. The book provides many examples of ethical problems along with recommended solutions. It also covers research management issues (e.g., special populations, IRB protocols, and authorship decisions).

National Academy Press has published an online book in association with the National Academy of Sciences, the National Academy of Engineering, and the Institute of Health. The book is entitled, *On Being a Scientist: Responsible Conduct in Research* and presents concerns for ethical behavior in research from across disciplines. It can be found at: http://www.nap.edu/readingroom/books/obas/

An online article of interest from the American Association for the Advancement of Science addresses the unique ethical concerns associated with internet-based research. The article is available at: http://www.aaas.org/spp/sfrl/projects/intres/main.htm

WEB RESOURCES
This site from the National Institutes of Health is entitled *Human Participant Protections Education for Research Teams*. It is a brief web tutorial on ethics that is intended for researchers. Five modules are included in the tutorial with careful attention paid to the historical basis of ethical guidelines and concerns for disclosure, confidentiality, and informed consent. Each module ends in a brief quiz, and completion of all modules results in certification of course completion that can be submitted with IRB protocols. The course also represents an effective homework assignment for Methods students. http://cme.nci.nih.gov/

Although the text lists this site from the APA Ethics Office as a web resource, it merits highlighting here since it includes links to several important documents that students should students. While the text does a good job of summarizing the major APA ethical guidelines for research with human and animal participants, it is often more revealing to review the original sources. Complete sets of guidelines for research involving human and animal participants are included as links. A link to the current draft of revisions to the ethics code also is provided, as are APA position statements concerning animal research and services by telephone and the Internet.
www.apa.org/ethics

Although research ethics often seems like commonsense, there are numerous examples of ethical violations. Recent examples of unethical research practices can be found at http://www.web-miner.com/researchethics.htm

RESEARCH METHODS WORKSHOPS

Two *Research Methods Workshops* are particularly relevant to information covered in this chapter. The workshop on *Ethical Issues* allows you to identify ways in which research can insure the benefits of research. The tutorial also covers investigator responsibilities and the importance of assessing risks to participants (including practice with a provided research example). Issues pertaining to the use of deception and minimizing risk are briefly reviewed. A review of the basic elements of consent forms, general privacy issues in research, and how to ethically summarize results is also provided. The second tutorial, *Effective Debriefing,* covers the disclosure of deception during the debriefing process, as well as when and what information should be disclosed. Brief mention is made of the fact that researchers can effectively ask some additional questions during debriefing to gather more information that is pertinent to their study. The workshop also discusses the importance of having a script to guarantee coverage of the necessary topics during debriefing and affords students valuable practice in generating a debriefing script from a sample study. Wadsworth's *Research Methods Workshops* can be found at: http://psychology.wadsworth.com/workshops/.

Chapter 13

Interpreting the Results of Research

SUMMARY
1. Interpreting Specific Results
   1.1. the problem of scale-attenuation
       1.1.1. **scale-attenuation effects** include
           1.1.1.1. **ceiling effects** occur when performance measures cluster near the upper
                   end of the scale, suggesting that true performance may exceed the upper
                   limits of the measurement scale
           1.1.1.2. **floor effects** occur when performance measures cluster near the lower
                   end of the scale, suggesting that true performance may be lower than the
                   lower limits of the measurement scale
       1.1.2. Scale-attenuation distorts the results, and may suggest the presence of an
               interaction when there is none
       1.1.3. Scarborough's experiment on the difference between visual and auditory
               presentation on retention was used to illustrate scale-attenuation effects
       1.1.4. possible scale-attenuation effects may be revealed by pilot research which
               may suggest that the difficulty of the experimental task should be increased (for
               ceiling effects) or reduced (for floor effects)
   1.2. Regression Artifacts
       1.2.1. **regression artifact** or **regression to the mean** is a confounding factor
               resulting unreliable scores that fall close to the mean
           1.2.1.1. all measurements include some amount of random error
           1.2.1.2. when a group of people is measured, the extreme scores are likely to be
                   high or low in part because of this measurement error
           1.2.1.3. if these people were measured again, the pattern of random error would
                   be different
               1.2.1.3.1. this means that the new scores of the people who made extreme
                           scores on the first test would likely be closer to the group mean on
                           the second test
               1.2.1.3.2. the extreme scorers have *regressed toward the mean*
           1.2.1.4. regression artifacts are an important threat to the internal validity of
                   quasi-experiments when the nonequivalent control groups are formed on
                   the basis of matching participants on the basis of subject variables
               1.2.1.4.1. this problem is particularly dangerous when control participants
                           with extreme scores are selected to match people from a group with
                           a different mean
           1.2.1.5. regression in compensatory education

1.2.1.5.1.   Cicirelli and Granger's evaluation of the Head Start Program was considered with respect to regression artifacts
1.2.1.6. Whenever possible, participants should be randomly assigned to the treatment conditions
2.   Interpreting Patterns of Research
    2.1. reliability and replication
        2.1.1.   **test reliability** refers to consistency of measurements
        2.1.2.   **experimental reliability** refers to the consistency of results over **replications**
            2.1.2.1. types of replication
                2.1.2.1.1.   **direct replication** refers to repeating an experiment as closely as possible to the original
                2.1.2.1.2.   **systematic replication** deliberately modifies many factors believed to be irrelevant to the original results
                2.1.2.1.3.   **conceptual replication** attempts to replicate a finding in an entirely different way, by using a different operational definition of the concept
                2.1.2.1.4.   as we progress from direct to conceptual replication, we extend the external validity of the results
        2.1.3.   Luchin's **Einstellung** (or set) experiments were considered with respect to experimental reliability
    2.2. Converging Operations
        2.2.1.   converging operations are a set of two or more operations the eliminate alternative concepts that might explain a set of experimental results
            2.2.1.1. help provide validity for concepts and hypotheses
            2.2.1.2. help eliminate alternative explanations
        2.2.2.   Examples of research that used converging operations include
            2.2.2.1. alternative explanations (i.e., demand characteristics and priming) to motivated search of memory for the reasons for success were eliminated using converging operations (Sanitiosa, Kunda, and Fong, 1990)
                ■   research on **personal space** in which the concept was defined by very different operational definitions (Kinzel, 1970)

LEARNING THE TERMINOLOGY

Ceiling Effects When performance is at the upper limit of the scale. A type of scale-attenuation effect (p. 301)

Conceptual replications Attempt to demonstrate an experimental phenomenon with an entirely new paradigm or set of experimental conditions (p.313)

Converging operations A set of related lines of investigation that all support a common conclusion (p. 315)

Direct replication Repeating an experiment as closely as possible to determine whether the same results will be obtained (p. 313)

Einstellung The effect of expectancy on cognition; for example, if the people solve problems in one particular way, they will often approach new problems in the same way even when the original strategy is no longer effective (p. 311)

Experimental reliability The extent to which the experimental results can be replicated (p. 310)

Floor effects When performance is at the bottom of the scale. A type of scale-attenuation effect (p. 301)

Personal space The "invisible bubble" surrounding a person that protects one from social encroachments (p. 317)

Regression artifact An artifact in the measurement of change on a variable when groups of subjects who scored at the extremes on the variable are tested again (p. 305)

Regression to the mean Tendency for extreme measures on some variable to be closer to the group mean when re-measured, due to unreliability of measurement (p. 305)

Replication The replication of an earlier experiment to duplicate its findings. Also the term used to describe experimental reliability (p. 311)

Scale-attenuation effects Difficulties in interpreting results when performance on the dependent variable is either nearly perfect (ceiling) or nearly lacking altogether (floor) (p. 301)

Systematic Replication Repeating an experiment while varying numerous factors considered to be irrelevant to the phenomenon to see if it will survive these changes (p. 313)

Test reliability Giving the same test twice in succession over a short interval to see if the scores are stable, or reliable; generally expressed as a correlation between scores on the tests (p. 310)

KEY TERM MATCHING

1.	
____ conceptual replication	a. a threat to internal validity in matched-groups quasi-experiments
____ converging operations	
____ direct replication	b. deliberately changing factors believed to be irrelevant
____ regression artifact	
____ scale-attenuation effect	c. floor and ceiling effects

___ systematic replication	d. independent procedures that eliminate alternate explanations
	e. redoing an experiment under the original conditions
	f. using new operational definitions
2. ___ Einstellung ___ experimental reliability ___ personal space ___ regression to the mean ___ test reliability	a. area surrounding a person outside of which another person is not threatening b. consistency of measures c. established through replication d. extreme scorers on a test tend to score closer to the group average in a second test. e. response set

FILL-IN-THE-BLANK

1. Performance levels near either to the top or the bottom of the scale of the dependent variable are called _____-_____ effects.
2. _____ effects are observed when performance is nearly perfect, and _____ effects are observed when performance is almost nonexistent.
3. Researchers usually test small groups of _____ participants to determine whether ceiling or floor effects are going to be a problem in their research.
4. If a scale-attenuation problem exists, then one way to avoid this problem is to change the _____ of the task.
5. If people are given two successive tasks, and we find that those who scored high in test 1 tended to score somewhat lower on test 2, this would represent a statistical _____ to the _____.
6. Regression artifacts occur because all psychological measurements are subject to a certain amount of _____.
7. In the Westinghouse-Ohio study, the two samples of children probably came from different _____.
8. The best method for eliminating confounding factors is _____ _____ of participants to conditions.
9. Two key factors for ensuring reliability are a _____ number of observations and a _____ result.
10. An unreliable test is also an _____ test.
11. Many experimental psychologists find _____ reliability more convincing than statistical reliability.
12. In Luchin's water-jar problem, the (experimental/control) _____ group received all 11 of the problems to be solved.
13. In a _____ _____, an experiment is repeated as closely as possible, and with as few changes as possible in the method.

14. In a _____ replication, many factors that the investigator considers irrelevant to the phenomenon of interest are changed in the replication.
15. _____ _____ are a set of two or more operations that eliminate alternative concepts that might explain a set of experimental results.
16. In Kinzel's (1970) study on personal space, the dependent variable was _____.
17. Barefoot, Hoople and McClay (1792) found that _____ people stopped to drink water when the experimenter sat close to the fountain than when he sat far from the fountain.

MULTIPLE CHOICE
1. Scale attenuation effects are observed when
   a. subjects fail to show any savings from one learning trial to the next.
   b. performance is virtually perfect or virtually nonexistent.
   c. recognition performance is superior to recall performance.
   d. recency effects are larger than primary effects.

3. Which of the following statements best summarizes the problem of scale attenuation effects?
   a. There is no such thing as perfectly good or perfectly bad performance.
   b. The size of the intervals of a dependent measure are unequal when you approach the extreme ends of the scale.
   c. It is impossible to determine whether there are differences among experimental conditions when performance is polarized at either the high or low end of the scale of the dependent measure.
   d. Most of the dependent measures used to study memory are relatively unconstrained and thus allow for easy interpretation of performance levels.

4. One might reduce problems of ceiling and floor effects by
   a. avoiding the use of tasks that are too easy.
   b. avoiding the use of tasks that are too difficult.
   c. testing pilot subjects to make sure that performance on a task will not be near the extremes of the scale.
   d. all of the above

5. Statistical regression to the mean refers to the fact that
   a. when people are tested twice, those with high scores on test 1 tend to have scores that are closer to the group mean on test 2.
   b. in psychology most test scores tend to fall close to the mean, with few very deviant scores.
   c. in an experiment employing repeated tests, subjects who perform poorly on the early test(s) will tend to do better on the later test(s).
   d. both a and c

6. Quasi-experimental designs are particularly susceptible to bias due to measurement error because
   a. there are no control variables.
   b. subjects are not randomly assigned to groups.
   c. the experimental and control groups are not matched prior to the introduction of the independent variable.
   d. all of the above

7. Two students take a History exam. The first student has an A average but makes a C on the test whereas the second student who had a D average makes an A on the exam. Assuming that these discrepancies are due to measurement error, it is likely that the first student will make a(n) _____ and the second student will make a(n) _____ on the next exam.
   a. C; A
   b. A; C
   c. C; C
   d. C; B

8. The reliability of a test refers to
   a. whether the test measures what it is intended to measure.
   b. how well the test can predict future performance.
   c. how stable scores are across testings of the same subjects.
   d. how stable scores are across different groups.

9. The basic issue regarding reliability of experimental results is:
   a. whether we can draw a conclusion regarding a causal relation between the independent and dependent variables.
   b. if the experiment were repeated would the results be the same as were found the first time.
   c. whether the conclusions are warranted, given the design of the experiment.
   d. the presence or absence of possible confounding factors.

10. *Einstellung* is the German word for _____.
   a. problem
   b. experimentation
   c. reactivity
   d. set

11. In a _____ we replicate a phenomenon or concept, but in a way that differs from the original demonstration.
   a. systematic replication
   b. paradigmatic replication
   c. conceptual replication
   d. indirect replication

12. Converging operations
   a. are a set of two or more operations used to eliminate alternative explanations for a set of experimental results.
   b. provide more than one way of arriving at an experimental conclusion.
   c. allow psychologists to distinguish between two competing explanations of an effect.
   d. all of the above

13. Which of the following is true?
   a. Converging operations are useful in validating mental constructs.
   b. Converging operations are experimental operations that produce different results.
   c. Converging operations are a set of two or more operational definitions.
   d. both a and c.

14. Prisoners were found to have larger personal space bubbles when they were classified as
   a. nonviolent.
   b. violent.
   c. depressed.
   d. homosexual.

15. Kinzel (1970) found that violent prisoners have
    a. larger personal space bubbles than nonviolent prisoners.
    b. smaller personal space bubbles than nonviolent prisoners.
    c. a larger personal space area in front than in behind.
    d. both a and c

16. In approaching a violent prisoner, you would be more likely to invade his personal space if you approached from the prisoner's
    a. left side.
    b. right side.
    c. front.
    d. rear.

TRUE-FALSE
1. There is no way to avoid ceiling and floor effects in psychological research; we just have to learn to interpret them carefully.
2. Scale attenuation effects can hide actual differences that may exist between experimental conditions.
3. Scale attenuation effects can be avoided by effectively manipulating task difficulty.
4. Regression to the mean is an experimental artifact.
5. Regression artifacts would never be a problem if measurement error could be eliminated completely.
6. Regression artifacts pose very few problems as long as subjects are drawn from different underlying populations.
7. Quasi-experimental designs are less susceptible to bias than true experiments because of regression to the mean.
8. If a test is reliable then we know that it measures what it was intended to measure.
9. Many psychologists find experimental reliability less convincing than statistical reliability.
10. A direct replication involves simply repeating an experiment as closely as possible with as few changes in the method as possible.
11. Kinzel (1970) found that violent prisoners have larger personal space "bubbles" than do nonviolent prisoners.
12. Converging operations are a set of two or more operations that suggest alternative explanations for an experimental result.
13. An experimenter can be satisfied that he or she has eliminated all alternative explanations of an experimental result if two converging operations have led to the same conclusion.

RESEARCH DILEMMA

One strategy used to describe those who are successful in sports is to examine elite athletes. Since you have a particular interest in rowing, you travel to the U.S. Olympic training facility and interview all the rowing athletes there. Based upon your interviews, you develop a questionnaire (ORSS – the Olympic Rowing Success Scale) that reflects the characteristics the athletes described as important for high level competition in rowing. You then administer the questionnaire to the athletes and wait to see which rowers make the Olympic team as a measure of criterion validity. You find a somewhat non-significant correlation of .22 between your questionnaire and the rowing times at the Olympic trials. You are not satisfied with this result and decide to reconstruct the questionnaire. What are some factors you should consider?

ANSWER KEY

Key Term Matching
1. f,d,e,a,c,b
2. e, c, a, d, b

Fill-in-the-blank
1. scale attenuation (p. 301)
2. ceiling, floor (p. 301)
3. pilot (p. 303)
4. difficulty (p. 304)
5. regression, mean (p. 306)
6. error (p. 306)
7. populations (p. 307)
8. random assignment (p. 309)
9. large, repeatable (p. 310)
10. invalid (p. 310)
11. experimental (p.310)
12. experimental (p.311)
13. direct, replication (p. 313)
14. systematic (p. 313)
15. converging operations (p. 315)
16. proximity a prisoner would tolerate another person (p. 317)
17. fewer (p. 318-319)

Multiple Choice
1. b (p. 301)	7. c (p. 310)
2. c (p. 301)	8. b (p. 310)
3. d (p. 303)	9. d (p. 311)
4. d (p. 305)	10. c (p. 313)
5. b (p. 306)	11. d (p. 314)
6. b (p. 306)	12. d (p. 315)

13. b (p. 317)   15. d (p. 318)
14. a (p. 318)

True False
1. F (p. 303)   8. T (p. 310)
2. T (p. 305)   9. F (p. 310)
3. T (pp. 204-305)   10. T (p. 313)
4. F (p. 305)   11. T (p. 317)
5. T (p. 306)   12. T (p. 315)
6. F (p. 307)   13. F (p. 316)
7. F (p. 307)

Research Dilemma
There are a variety of things you should evaluate when reconstructing the questionnaire. For instance, wording, framing and item order can all influence how people respond to questions. In addition, if the items have high face validity (i.e., it is clear what the items are asking for), there may be participant reactivity causing all the rowers to respond is a favorable manner. However, before reconstructing the questionnaire, it may be wise to administer the questionnaire to rowers who did not qualify for the Olympic trials. It may be that by basing your questionnaire on these elite athletes and then giving them the questionnaire you have a restricted range in responses that may underestimate criterion validity of your instrument. By testing a more diverse sample in regard to ability you should increase the variability on your questionnaire. You can then examine whether or not the rowers who make the Olympic trials are different from those that do not.

FURTHER READINGS
This article provides a detailed definition of converging operations and discusses its implications for advances in psychological research. Specifically, the article reveals the advantages of combining results from multiple disciplines and paradigms. The problems associated with the reliance on a single approach also are discussed.

Sternberg, R. J., & Grigorenko, E. L. (2001). Unified psychology. *American Psychologist, 56*(12), 1069-1079.

Conducting and interpreting statistical analyses can sometimes be confusing. However, do not be discouraged if this happens. You might be surprised to know that researchers experience some difficulties as well. Zuckerman et al (1993) found that only 59 percent of 551 research psychologists correctly answered a 5-question survey covering reliability and Type I and II errors, interactions, contrast analysis, and power and effect size.

Zuckerman, M., Hodgins, H. S., Zuckerman, A., & Rosenthal, R. (1993). Contemporary issues in the analysis of data: A survey of 551 psychologists. *Psychological Science, 4,* 49-53.

A good resource is the *Dictionary of Statistics and Methodology*. This book allows you to quickly find information about statistics and design topics.

Vogt, P. (1993). *Dictionary of statistics and methodology: A nontechnical guide for the social sciences*. Newbury Park, CA: Sage.

WEB RESOURCES
http://www.junkscience.com/news/apwilmut.htm,
http://www.junkscience.com/news/wilmut2.htm and
http://www.junkscience.com/news/wilmut3.htm
The above addresses are archived links within Junkscience.com, a site that claims to print "all the junk that's fit to debunk". The site's archives have many examples of failures to replicate results that could be used to help students realize the importance of replication to research progress. The pages cited above are online versions of newspaper articles and a journal note about the replicability, and thus the validity, of Ian Wilmut's original research on cloning sheep.

RESEARCH METHODS WORKSHOPS
Now that you have been exposed to the various concerns, methods, and strategies for conducting research, the *Common Mistakes in Student Research* tutorial will provide a good review of the text. The workshop reviews difficulties that students frequently have when first getting involved in the research process. An extended example is used of students interested in conformity, and specifically, replicating Asch's (1955) classic line-judgment studies. For each potential mistake, you are prompted to provide suggestions for how to avoid the problem(s) in the extended example and/or reflect on the lessons learned from the student research team. Wadsworth's *Research Methods Workshops* can be found at: http://psychology.wadsworth.com/workshops/.

Chapter 14

Presenting Research Results

SUMMARY

1. How to Write a Research Report
   1.1. The self-correcting nature of science requires good data to be published
   1.2. The *Publication Manual of the American Psychological Society* is the official arbiter of style for most journals in psychology
   1.3. Format
      1.3.1. The cover page of the copy manuscript contains
         1.3.1.1. the title
         1.3.1.2. author's name and affiliation
         1.3.1.3. the **running head** which will appear at the top of each page in the published article
         1.3.1.4. **short title** which identifies each page of the manuscript during editing
      1.3.2. the **abstract** appears on the second page
      1.3.3. the full title appears on the third page, followed by the **introduction**
      1.3.4. the **method** section immediately follows the introduction
         1.3.4.1. the use of side headings *Participants* , *Apparatus,* and *Procedure* will help guide the reader
      1.3.5. the **results** section immediately follows the method
      1.3.6. the **discussion** section immediately follows the results
      1.3.7. references begin on a separate page
      1.3.8. any author notes or footnotes follow the references on a separate page
      1.3.9. Data tables mentioned in the results section follow the footnote
         1.3.9.1. captions to figures appear next, followed by
         1.3.9.2. figures, one to each page, which complete the report
   1.4. Style
      1.4.1. transitions between sections should be smooth and straightforward
      1.4.2. titles should be short, and mention the independent and dependent variables
      1.4.3. avoid too much detail in the abstract
      1.4.4. the introduction should review relevant information and justify the present experiment to the reader
      1.4.5. the method section should present enough information so that a reader could replicate your study
      1.4.6. the results section should state clearly what was found

1.4.7. the discussion should relate your results to the question that motivated the research

1.4.8. the APA publication manual recommends that the writer

1.4.8.1. use the precise word,

1.4.8.2. avoid ambiguity,

1.4.8.3. order the presentation of ideas, and

1.4.8.4. consider the reader

1.4.9. use the present tense for the current experiment, and the past tense in review earlier work. Check for agreement between plural and collective nouns and their verbs

1.4.9.1. do not overuse the passive or the active voice

2. How to Publish an Article

2.1. articles are submitted to the editor of an appropriate journal

2.2. the editor sends the article to reviewers, who provide useful comments to the author

2.3. the publication process usually takes over a year

3. How to Give an Oral Presentation

3.1. content

3.1.1. most oral presentations are limited to about 15 minutes with a two to three minute question period

3.1.2. avoid unnecessary detail

3.1.2.1. the introduction should include your research question and why it is important

3.1.2.1.1. define terms as needed for audience (generally terms that are not generally known)

3.1.2.1.2. briefly review literature

3.1.2.1.3. state hypothesis

3.1.2.2. describe how the study was conducted

3.1.2.2.1. include the independent and dependent variables

3.1.2.2.2. do not spent too much time on procedural details

3.1.2.3. present results

3.1.2.3.1. use tables and/or figures

3.1.2.3.2. do not just report numbers but state the findings in general terms

3.1.2.4. restate hypothesis and outline conclusions

3.2. style

3.2.1. memorize the first and last sentences of talk

3.2.2. do not read the talk

3.2.2.1. make an outline to speak from

3.2.3. use appropriate visual aids

3.2.3.1. use a large font

3.2.3.2. avoid clutter or too much detail on a single overhead or slide

168

3.2.4.   practice the talk
4. How to Give a Poster Presentation
    4.1. posters provide the same details as a paper but in an abbreviated form
    4.2. they are prepared before a conference and placed on a poster board
        4.2.1.   can use PowerPoint or similar program to create poster
            4.2.1.1. print as one large poster or in segments on multiple sheets of paper
            4.2.1.2. should have handouts of the poster
        4.2.2.   be prepared to summarize your research (or go through your poster) in one to two minutes

Learning the Terminology

Abstract. Short summary at the beginning of a journal article that informs the reader about the results (p. 326)

APA format. The journal article format specified by the American Psychological Association (APA) (p. 328)

Copy manuscript. The pre-print version of a research report; that is, it is a manuscript that has not yet been printed in a technical journal (p. 325)

Discussion. A section of a technical paper in which the author draws theoretical conclusions by examining, interpreting, and qualifying the results (p. 327)

Figure captions. Descriptions of figures that appear on a page separate from the figures that appear on a page separate from the figures in a copy manuscript (p. 327)

Figures. Graphical presentations of data in the results sections of a research report (p. 326)

Introduction. The portion of a technical paper that specifies the problem to be studied and tells why it is important. (p.326)

Method. A section of a technical paper that describes in detail the operations performed by the experimenter (p. 336)

Reference. Found at the end of a technical paper; only articles cited in the text are included in the reference section (p. 327)

Results. A section of a technical paper that tells what happened in the research (p. 326)

Running head. The heading that appears at the top of the page of a published article (p. 325)

Short title. The first few words of the title, which appears at the top of each page of the copy manuscript (p. 325)

Tables . A non-graphical was of summarizing data in a technical paper. Summary values of the dependent variable are presented under headings describing the levels of the independent variable (p. 326)

Title. Provides an idea of the contents of an article or technical paper and usually states only the dependent and independent variables (p. 325)

KEY TERM MATCHING

1.	a. between cover page and introduction
___ abstract	b. gives enough detail to allow a replication of the experiment
___ APA format	c. guide that standardizes order and context of an article
___ copy manuscript	d. heading that appears at the top of each page in published article
___ discussion	e. heading that appears at the top of each page in the copy manuscript
___ figures	f. names independent and dependent variables
___ introduction	g. only section of article that does not have a heading
___ materials	h. subheading in method section
___ method	i. the final page or pages of the copy manuscript
___ running head	j. version of the article prepared to facilitate editing
___ short title	k. where the results are interpreted
___ title	

FILL-IN-THE-BLANK
1. In an APA-style report, the cover sheet includes

_____

_____
2. Page two of a research report contains the _____.
3. The title of a research project appears on the third page and immediately precedes the _____ section.
4. Any published reports cited in a paper are listed in the _____.
5. The biggest stylistic problem in most research reports is _____ from one section to the next.
6. The _____ tense should be used in the Introduction and Method section and the _____ tense is generally acceptable for the Results and Discussion sections.

7. Overuse of the _____ voice might be stuffy, while overuse of the _____ voice emphasizes the researcher rather than the study.
8. One is obliged to publish good data because of the _____ _____ nature of the scientific enterprise.
9. When giving an oral presentation, it is better to speak from a _____ rather than to _____ the paper.
10. "The participant completed the task" is an example of _____ voice.
11. "The task was completed by the participant" is an example of _____ voice.
12. _____ and _____ are not included in the body of the paper but are placed at the end of the manuscript.
13. References need to follow _____ format.
14. When making a presentation, you should always state your _____ _____ and which it is _____.
15. Perhaps the most important quality of a paper is _____.

MULTIPLE CHOICE
1. Which type of heading appears in entirely in capital letters on the first pate of the copy manuscript? This heading will appear at the top of the published article.
   a. keyword(s)
   b. running head
   c. author(s)
   d. title

2. Which subsection of a manuscript does have a heading by the same name?
   a. abstract
   b. introduction
   c. method
   d. discussion

3. Which of the following is NOT typically a subsection of the Method section?
   a. participants
   b. procedure
   c. material
   d. consent

4. Which section of the method typically discusses compensation for involvement in the study (e.g., paid participation versus partial fulfillment of course requirements)?
   a. apparatus
   b. procedure
   c. participants
   d. methods

5. In the results section, you should
   a. state what happened when you examined the variables
   b. state what variables you will be examining
   c. state how you examined the variables
   d. state what the effects of the variables mean

6. In scientific writing it is generally important to
   a. include extra details to keep the reader interested
   b. refer to yourself in the paper as "I" or "we"
   c. use the active voice only
   d. use consistent terminology

7. Which statement below is true of the publication process?
   a. average rejection rates of journals are greater than 70 percent
   b. authors retain all copyright privileges
   c. authors are paid for accepted papers
   d. the final decision about a manuscript submitted for publication is the reviewer's

8. Accepted papers that are in the form that they will appear in the journal, but are not published yet, are called
   a. copy manuscripts
   b. editorial manuscripts
   c. galley proofs
   d. submissions

9. The typical acceptable manuscript gets published as a journal article within _____ after it has been written and submitted.
   a. several weeks
   b. several months
   c. about one year
   d. three to five years

10. As a general rule, verbal presentations of a poster should be
    a. as detailed as a written submission to a journal
    b. not needed since the research is presented visually
    c. about the same as an oral presentation
    d. only about two minutes

11. References should follow which formatting style?
    a. AMA
    b. APA
    c. MLA
    d. Chicago

12. Figures are placed on a separate page
    a. so that they can be looked at side-by-side with the text
    b. to minimize word processing problems
    c. to increase submission length
    d. to facilitate the typesetting process

13. The discussion section should
    a. predict results
    b. direct the reader to data that seem most relevant to the purpose of the research
    c. present enough information to allow for replication
    d. show how results relate to hypotheses

14. The method section should
    a. predict results
    b. direct the reader to data that seem most relevant to the purpose of the research
    c. present enough information to allow for replication
    d. show how results relate to hypotheses

15. The result section should
    a. predict results
    b. direct the reader to data that seem most relevant to the purpose of the research
    c. present enough information to allow for replication
    d. show how results relate to hypotheses

TRUE-FALSE
1. The title usually contains the main research implication.
2. The introduction should always end with a question.
3. The results section should conclude with a summary of the purpose for the study and the results.
4. Passive voice is preferred in the sciences.
5. You should be prepared for approximately 15 minutes for a poster presentation.

EXPERIMENTAL DILEMMA
Your professor is impressed with the research project you completed for the Research Methods course. He suggests that you present your study at a research conference. You as whether or not you should request to make an oral presentation or a poster presentation. Your professor suggests that you should make a poster presentation, "especially as a first time presenter", but does not offer any other explanation. Why do you think he would make such a recommendation?

ANSWER KEY

Key Term Matching
1. a, c, j, k, i, g, h, b, d, e, f

Fill in the Blank
1. title, author, affiliation, running head, short title (p. 325)
2. abstract (p. 326)
3. introduction (p. 326)
4. references (p. 327)
5. transition (p. 350)
6. past, present (p. 352)
7. passive, active (p. 352)
8. self-correcting (p. 325)
9. outline, read (p. 356)
10. active (p. 353)
11. passive (p. 353)
12. tables, figures (p. 326)
13. APA (p. 352)
14. research question, interesting (p. 355)
15. clarity (p. 351)

Multiple Choice

1. b (p. 325)
2. b (p. 326)
3. d (p. 350)
4. c (pp. 350-351)
5. a (p. 351)
6. d (p. 353)
7. a (p. 354)
8. c (p. 354)
9. c (p. 354)
10. d (p. 357)
11. b (p. 327)
12. d (p. 327)
13. d (p. 352)
14. c (p. 352)
15. b (p. 352)

True-False
1. F (p. 350)
2. F (p. 350)
3. T (p. 351)
4. F (p. 353)
5. F (p. 357)

Experimental Dilemma
There are several reasons why a poster presentation might be preferred over an oral presentation for your first conference. Two key reasons are presented here. First, posters are presented in large rooms where a number of researchers present their posters at the

same time. You are not the focus of attention in the same way as you are when making an oral presentation. This is particularly important for first time presenters since it tends to reduce presentation anxiety. Second, with a poster you make several two minute presentations instead of one 15 minute presentation. This means that you get to interact with more people about your research. The more people you interact with the more feedback you receive about your research which will hopefully generate additional research ideas.

FURTHER READINGS
As the title suggests, this is APA's student workbook on APA style. It is designed to expedite the learning of APA format in a user-friendly way through the application of elements from the publication manual to examples.

Gelfand, H., & Walker, C. J. (2001). *Mastering APA style: Student's workbook and training guide*. Washington, DC: American Psychological Association.

This guide for student writers separately discusses each section of the APA-style paper in order to familiarize students with the critical elements that are unique to each section. The book is presented in a workbook-like format with several brief writing exercises in each chapter. Also included is a section on how to develop a poster presentation, and new to this edition is a section on how to write literature review papers. The text also comes bundled with *InfoTrac* to provide students online access to articles that could provide the basis for further writing exercises and literature searches.

Szuchman, L. T. (2002). *Writing with style: APA style made easy* (2nd ed.). Pacific Grove, CA: Wadsworth.

If you are interested in learning more about the publication process, the edited book by Sternberg (2000) below is an excellent resource. Leading researchers contributed to the book by addressing different parts of the writing and publication process. You'll read about tips for writing each section of a paper as well as how to write to your referees, respond to the editorial decision about your paper, and rewrite your paper based on reviewer comments.

Sternberg, R. J. (Ed.). (2000). *Guide to publishing in psychology journals*. New York: Cambridge University Press.

WEB RESOURCES
This section of the writing style portion of the American Psychological Association's web site is devoted to summarizing the major changes from the fourth to the fifth editions of the *Publication Manual of the American Psychological Association*. Separate links are

provided to changes in each chapter of the manual, including content and style, as well as reference and manuscript preparation with sample papers. Additional links include style tips, a guide to electronic references, and answers to frequently asked questions. http://www.apastyle.org/fifthchanges.html

APA has also created a list of Style Tips based on common questions about APA Style. The list is found at http://www.apastyle.org/previoustips.html.

A number of helpful links for material covering APA Style as well as general writing considerations can be accessed from the following web page: http://www.tulsa.oklahoma.net/~jnichols/Writing.html

Psi Chi, the national honor society for psychology, has a number of helpful links for writing, presenting, and publishing research.
- Information and general guidelines for preparing a paper or poster conference presentation can be found at http://www.psichi.org/content/conventions/tips.asp and http://www.psichi.org/pubs/articles/article_91.asp
- Information regarding outlets for student research can be found at http://www.psichi.org/pubs/articles/article_92.asp
- A helpful article showing how to use the APA 5th ed. Publication style is available at http://www.psichi.org/pubs/articles/article_458.asp

RESEARCH METHODS WORKSHOPS
The *APA Style* tutorial provides a description of the APA Publication Manual and provides links to Publication Manual resources. The workshop concludes with an exercise in editing according APA style. Wadsworth's *Research Methods Workshops* can be found at: http://psychology.wadsworth.com/workshops/.

Appendix A

Descriptive Statistics

Summary

1. Descriptive Statistics: Telling It Like It Is
    1.1. **Frequency Distributions**
        1.1.1.   are graphs that show how often scores of particular magnitudes appear in a group of scores
        1.1.2.   Score values are plotted on the abscissa (or X axis)
        1.1.3.   Frequencies are plotted on the ordinate (or Y axis)
        1.1.4.   Examples of frequency distributions include the
            1.1.4.1. **Histogram** - or bar chart
                1.1.4.1.1. Vertical bars are drawn for each score value in the sample range, or for groups of score values
                1.1.4.1.2. The height of these bars is made to be proportional to the number of scores that fall in the range that the bar represents
            1.1.4.2. **Frequency polygon** - a frequency distribution made by connecting the midpoints of the bars in a histogram
    1.2. Measures of **Central Tendency**
        1.2.1.   indicate the center of a distribution of scores, i.e. they indicate the most "typical" score in a group
        1.2.2.   Example of measures of central tendency
            1.2.2.1. the **mean** is
                1.2.2.1.1. the most commonly used measure of central tendency
                1.2.2.1.2. the arithmetic average of the scores in the sample
                1.2.2.1.3. the measure most strongly influenced by extreme scores
            1.2.2.2. the **median** is
                1.2.2.2.1. the middlemost score in a group; the number of scores exceeded by the median is the same as the number of scores that the median exceeds
                1.2.2.2.2. the median is often used when there are extreme scores in the sample
            1.2.2.3. the **mode** is
                1.2.2.3.1. the value of the most frequent score
                1.2.2.3.2. rarely reported in psychological research
    1.3. Measures of Dispersion
        1.3.1.   indicate how much scores in a sample are spread out about the center
        1.3.2.   the **range** is
            1.3.2.1. the simplest measure of dispersion

177

1.3.2.2. the difference between the highest and lowest scores in a sample

1.3.2.3. rarely used since it is based entirely on the extreme scores in a sample

1.3.3. the **mean deviation** is

1.3.3.1. a useful measure of dispersion

1.3.3.2. the average absolute amount by which scores differ from the mean

1.3.3.3. rarely used

1.3.4. the **variance** is

1.3.4.1. the sum of the squared deviations from the mean, divided by the number of scores

1.3.4.2. employed in inferential statistics

1.3.5. the **standard deviation** is

1.3.5.1. the square root of the variance

1.3.5.2. the most widely used measure of dispersion

2. The **Normal Distribution**

2.1. is a frequency distribution commonly found in psychological data

2.2. In a normal distribution,

2.2.1. the mean, median, and mode all coincide

2.2.2. the scores are symmetrically distributed about the mean

2.2.3. the inflection points lie exactly one standard deviation from the mean

2.2.4. approximately 68% of the scores fall between -1 and +1 standard deviation from the mean, 96% between -2 and +2 standard deviations, and 99.74% between -3 and +3 standard deviations

2.3. **Standard scores, or z-scores**

2.3.1. indicate how many standard deviations individual scores lie above or below the mean

2.3.2. z-scores are useful because they permit comparisons of measures of different characteristics

2.4. Correlation Coefficient

Key Term Matching

1.		a.	arithmetic average
		b.	average absolute difference between scores and the group mean
___	mean		
___	mean deviation	c.	difference between the highest and lowest scores
___	median	d.	middlemost score
___	mode	e.	most commonly used measure of dispersion
___	range	f.	number of standard deviations a

178

___ standard deviation	particular score lies from the mean
	g. sum of the squared deviations from the mean, divided by the number of scores
___ variance	
___ z-score	h. value of the most frequent score

2.
___ frequency distribution	a. commonly observed shape of a frequency distribution for psychological data
___ frequency polygon	b. constructed by connecting the midpoints of the bars in a bar graph
___ histogram	c. frequencies are indicated by the heights of vertical bars
___ normal distribution	d. general term for graphs that show how often particular score values occur in a sample

3.
___ measures of central tendency	a. indicate how different the scores are from each other in a sample
___ measures of dispersion	b. lies one standard deviation from the median in a normal distribution
___ inflection point	c. value of a most "typical" score in a sample

FILL-IN-THE-BLANK

1. The two main types of descriptive statistics are measures of _____ _____ and measures of _____.
2. One type of graphical representation of numerical data is a _____ or, bar graph.
3. The histogram and the _____ _____ are both examples of _____ distributions.
4. The most common measure of central tendency in psychological research is the _____.
5. The midpoint of the distribution is called the _____ while the most frequently occurring score in the distribution is called the _____.
6. A measure of central tendency that is relatively insensitive to extreme scores is the _____.
7. The difference between the highest and lowest scores in the distribution is called the _____.
8. When calculating the mean deviation, it is necessary to use the _____ value of the difference between each score and the group mean.

9. The _____ of a distribution is defined as the sum of the squared deviations from the mean divided by the number of scores.
10. The square root of the variance gives us the _____ _____ of the distribution.
11. The formula for the variance is $s^2 = $ _____
12. Psychologists typically present the _____ and the _____ _____ when describing a set of data.
13. A useful property of the normal curve is that a specific _____ of the scores fall under each part of the curve.
14. If two normal distributions have different means and variances then one way to compare scores across these two distributions is to convert the scores to _____ scores or _____ scores.
15. If we calculate the difference between an individual score and the mean of the distribution from which the score was taken, and then divide this difference by the standard deviation of the distribution, the resulting score represents a _____ score.

MULTIPLE CHOICE

1. Descriptive statistics
    a. summarize experimental observations.
    b. tell which data are important.
    c. indicate which differences are reliable.
    d. all of the above

2. The mean is:
    a. the same as the arithmetic average.
    b. the middle score.
    c. the most common score.
    d. the standard score.
    e. the extreme score.

3. The median is:
    a. the sum of scores divided by the number of scores.
    b. the most frequent score.
    c. the midpoint of the distribution of scores.
    d. the range of scores.

4. The primary reason the median is used is because
    a. it is the most useful measure of central tendency.
    b. it has the property of being insensitive to extreme scores.
    c. it has the property of accurately reflecting the range of scores.
    d. almost all inferential statistics are based on it.

5. The _____ is the most frequent score in a distribution.
    a. mode
    b. median
    c. mean
    d. range

6. What is the mode of this distribution?   1 3 4 4 6 9 11 12 15
    a. 4
    b. 6
    c. 7.2
    d. 14

7. The simplest measure of dispersion in a group of scores is the:
    a. mode.
    b. range.
    c. standard deviation.
    d. variance.
    e. z-score

8. A defining characteristic of the mean is that
    a. as n increases, the mean increases.
    b. the sum of the deviations of scores about the mean is always zero.
    c. the mean deviation equals the mean divided by n.
    d. the mean is always less than the range.

9. The variance of a distribution is defined as the _____ divided by the number of scores.
    a. sum of the absolute deviations from the mean
    b. differences between the highest and lowest scores
    c. sum of the squared deviations from the mean
    d. sum of the absolute deviations from the median

10. The square root of the variance is the
    a. standard deviation.
    b. average deviation.
    c. mean deviation.
    d. sample deviation.

11. In describing an array of data, psychologists typically present two descriptive statistics, which are
    a. the median and variance.
    b. the median and standard deviation.
    c. the mean and the variance.
    d. the mean and the standard deviation.

12. Which of the following is a characteristic of the standard normal distribution?
    a. The mean, median, and mode are the same.
    b. The mean and median only are the same.
    c. The median and mode only are the same.
    d. The mean and mode only are the same.
    e. none of the above

13. Approximately what percentage of scores in a normal distribution fall between plus and minus one standard deviation from the mean?
    a. 17%
    b. 34%
    c. 68%
    d. 96%
    e. 99.7%

14. Approximately what percentage of scores in a normal distribution have z-values between -2.0 and +2.0?
    a. 17%
    b. 34%
    c. 68%
    d. 96%
    e. 99.7%

True False
1. Another name for a histogram is a frequency polygon.
2. The most common measure of central tendency in psychological research is the mean.
3. Extremely small or large scores have an effect on the mean, but not on the mode or median.
4. The mean of a set of scores has the property that the deviations from the mean add up to zero.
5. The standard deviation is simply the square root of the variance.
6. A property of the standard normal distribution is that the mean and the median are the same, but the mode is different.
7. A z-score is the difference between an individual score and the mean expressed in units of standard deviation.

ANSWERS
Key Term Matching
1. a, b, d, h, c, e, g, f
2. d, b, c, a
3. c, a, b

Fill-in-the-blank
1. Central tendency, dispersion; (pp. 361)
2. histogram; (p. 361)
3. frequency polygon, frequency; (p. 361)
4. mean; (p. 362)
5. median, mode; (p. 362, 363)
6. median; (p. 362)
7. range; (p. 363)
8. absolute; (p. 364)
9. variance; (p. 364)
10. standard deviation; (p. 364)
11. Variance=$(\Sigma(X-\text{Mean})^2)/n$ (p. 365)
12. mean, standard deviation; (p. 361)
13. proportion; (p. 368)
14. standard, z; (p. 369)
15. z; (p. 369)

Multiple Choice
1. a (p. 361)
2. a (p. 362)
3. c (p. 362)
4. b (p. 363)
5. a (p. 363)
6. a (p. 363)
7. b (p. 363)
8. b (p. 364)
9. c (p. 365)
10. a (p. 365)
11. d (p. 366)
12. a (p. 367)
13. c (p. 368)
14. d (p. 369)

True-False
1. F (p. 361)
2. T (p. 362)
3. T (p. 363)
4. T (p. 364)
5. T (p. 365)
6. F (p. 368)
7. T (p. 369)

WEB RESOURCES

There are a number of online statistics texts that you can refer to for statistical help.

Introductory Statistics: Concepts, Models, and Applications by David W. Stockburger at Southwest Missouri State University is a good introductory level resource.
http://www.psychstat.smsu.edu/sbk00.htm

Some more advanced concepts are covered in:

PA 765 Statnotes: An Online Textbook by G. David Garson at North Carolina State University
http://www2.chass.ncsu.edu/garson/pa765/statnote.htm

Electronic Statistics Textbook by StatSoft (makers of *Statistica*)
http://www.statsoft.com/textbook.stathome.html

You can also find information about presenting results at the following websites:
Psychology with Style: A Hypertext Writing Guide by Mark Plonksy at the University of Wisconsin – Stevens Point
http://www.uwsp.edu/psych/apa4b.htm

Reporting Common Statistics in APA Format written by Laura Little at the University of Washington
http://depts.washington.edu/psywc/handouts/pdf/stats.pdf

Reporting Statistics in APA Style by Jeffrey Kahn at Illinois State University
http://www.ilstu.edu/~jhkahn/apastats.html

The Online Writing Lab (OWL) at Purdue also has a relevant workshop tutorial:
http://owl.english.purdue.edu/workshops/hypertext/apa/parts/results.html

STATISTICS WORKSHOPS

In addition to the *Research Methods Workshops*, Wadsworth also has a number of online *Statistics Workshops*. A number of these workshops are relevant to this appendix. These workshops include:
- Scale of Measurement
- Central Tendency and Variability
- Sampling Distribution
- Choosing the Correct Statistical Test
- Bivariate Scatter Plots
- Correlation

You can find these workshops at http://psychology.wadsworth.com/workshops/.

Appendix B

Inferential Statistics

Summary

1. Statistical Reasoning
    1.1. Inferential statistics helps us decide whether a difference between treatment means is due to chance or to the effect of our independent variable
        1.1.1. Sampling
            1.1.1.1. A sample is a subset of the population to which we want to generalize our results
            1.1.1.2. Due to chance, different samples drawn from the population will have different means
            1.1.1.3. The sample means of many samples drawn from the same population will be normally distributed: the mean of the sample means will be very close to the population mean
            1.1.1.4. The variation (measured by the **standard error of the mean**) among the means of large samples drawn from a population is smaller than that of small samples. Hence, a single large sample is more likely to be representative of the population
        1.1.2. Testing Hypotheses
            1.1.2.1. The experimenter generates a research hypothesis that an independent variable will produce some effect on a dependent variable
            1.1.2.2. Data are collected, and some differences are found among the means of the treatment groups
            1.1.2.3. Inferential statistics are used to determine the probability of obtaining differences as large as these, if the **null hypothesis** were true. The null hypothesis
                1.1.2.3.1. states that any differences found among treatment means is due to chance or sampling error
            1.1.2.4. If the probability is smaller than **alpha** (a predetermined level of probability, often equal to .05) the null hypothesis is *rejected*, and **statistically reliable differences** are claimed
            1.1.2.5. Two types of errors can occur in hypothesis testing:
                1.1.2.5.1. a **type I error** is rejecting the null hypothesis then it is true. The frequency of this happening is a function of the alpha level
                1.1.2.5.2. a **type II error** is failing to reject the null hypothesis when it is false. The probability of a type II error can be reduced by increasing the size of the experimental groups

1.1.2.6. Hypothesis testing can be either directional or nondirectional
    1.1.2.6.1.   **Directional** research hypotheses predict the direction of the experimental effect. **One-tailed** statistical tests are used, which reduces the probability of type II errors, provided that the obtained difference is in the predicted direction. One tailed tests are used in applied research
    1.1.2.6.2.   **Nondirectional** research hypotheses do not specify the direction of the effect of an independent variable. **Two-tailed** statistical tests are used, that are sensitive to differences in either direction. This more conservative approach is usually used in basic research

2. Statistical Tests
  2.1. Tests for Differences Between Two Groups
    2.1.1.   Between-Subjects designs
      2.1.1.1. The **Mann-Whitney U test** is used with ordinal level data
      2.1.1.2. The **between-subjects t-test** is used with interval level data
    2.1.2.   Within-Subjects designs
      2.1.2.1. The **Wilcoxon signed-ranks test** is used with ordinal level data
      2.1.2.2. The **within-subjects t-test** is used with interval level data
      2.1.2.3. the **point-biserial** correlation (r_{pb}) can be used in conjunction with either t-test as a measure of the **magnitude of effect** of the independent variable
    2.1.3.   The Analysis of Variance (ANOVA)
      2.1.3.1. the **F-statistic** is a ratio of two independent estimates of the population variance
        2.1.3.1.1.   The estimate in the numerator is based on differences among the means of the various groups in the experiment. This will be large if the independent variables affect behavior
        2.1.3.1.2.   The estimate in the denominator is based on the spread of scores within each of the treatment groups. This should not be affected by the independent variable
        2.1.3.1.3.   According to the null hypothesis, the expected value of F is 1.0; if there are treatment effects, F will be larger than 1.0
        2.1.3.1.4.   The **one-way ANOVA** is used when there are more than two levels of a single independent variable, and a between-subject design is used
        2.1.3.1.5.   The within-subjects or **treatment X subjects ANOVA** is used for within-subjects designs involving a single independent variable
        2.1.3.1.6.   **Multifactor ANOVA**s are used for experiments with two or more independent variables.

Key Term Matching

1.

___ alpha level

___ directional test

___ nondirectional test

___ type-I error

___ type-II error

___ parameters

___ statistics

a. incorrectly rejecting the null hypothesis
b. inversely related to statistical power
c. measures of properties of populations
d. measures of properties of samples
e. probability criterion for statistical significance
f. research hypotheses predicts the direction of the effect of the independent variable
g. two-tailed test

2.

___ F-statistic

___ Mann-Whitney U test

___ multifactor ANOVA

___ standard error of the mean

___ Wilcoxon signed-ranks test

a. between-subjects nonparametric test
b. decreases as the sample size increases
c. A nonparametric test for two related groups
d. two or more independent variables
e. standard deviation of a distribution of sample means

Fill-in-the-blank

1. A complete set of measurements (or individual or objects) having some common observable characteristic is called a _____.
2. A subset of a population is called a _____.
3. If we conducted an experiment and then replicated that same experiment many times, the distribution of the resultant sample means would tend to be a _____ distribution.
4. The standard deviation of a distribution of sample means is called the _____ of the _____.
5. In general we want the standard error of the mean to be as _____ as possible. One way to do this is to _____ the size of the sample.
6. In testing hypotheses we pit the _____ hypothesis against the _____ hypothesis.

187

7. The null hypothesis predicts that _____

8. If we know the standard deviation of the population then we can find the standard error of the mean by dividing the population standard deviation by_____
_____

9. If you are told that an observed difference was significant at the .05 level of confidence then this means that_____

10. Rejecting the null hypothesis when it is actually true is called a Type _____ error, and the probability that this error is being made is indexed by the _____ level.

11. If we fail to reject the null hypothesis when it is in fact false, then we have committed a Type _____ error.

12. A conservative statistical test minimizes Type _____ errors.

13. The _____ of a test is the probability of rejecting the null hypothesis when it is actually false.

14. By increasing the _____ _____ we may increase the power of our test.

15. If the alternative hypothesis specifies the direction of the expected difference, then a _____-tailed test is used, but if the alternative hypothesis is nondirectional then a _____-tailed test is used.

16. Two-tailed tests are more _____ and _____ powerful than one-tailed tests.

17. A _____ statistical test is one that makes assumptions about the underlying population parameters of the samples on which the tests are performed.

18. In general _____ tests are less powerful than _____ tests employed in the same situation.

19. The Mann-Whitney U test is used to analyze data from a _____-subject design. The Wilcoxon signed-ranks test is used to analyze data from a _____-_____ design.

20. If a researcher used four levels of an independent variable and tested four separate groups of subjects, an appropriate statistical test for analyzing the data from this experiment would be a simple _____ _____ _____.

21. The F-test used in the analysis of variance is a ratio of the _____-groups variance estimate to the _____-groups variance estimate.

22. The null hypothesis predicts that the F-ratio should be _____.

23. In an experiment in which more than one factor is varied simultaneously the appropriate procedure for analyzing the results would be to use a _____ analysis of variance.

Multiple Choice

1. Inferential statistics are concerned with
a. the importance of data.
b. the meaning of data.
c. the reliability of data.
d. all of the above

2. Characteristics of a population of scores are called _____, while characteristics of a sample of scores drawn from a larger population are _____.
a. statistics; parameters
b. parameters; statistics
c. generalizations; data
d. inferences; facts

3. The distribution of sample means tends to be
a. normal.
b. exponential.
c. Poisson.
d. random.

4. The standard error of the mean is the
a. square root of the mean.
b. mean of a distribution of sample means
c. variance of a distribution of sample means
d. standard deviation of a distribution of sample means

5. The standard error of the mean represents the error we have in assuming that
a. the mean represents the sample mean.
b. the sample mean represents the population mean.
c. the standard deviation of the sample mean is accurate.
d. the standard deviation of the population mean is accurate.

6. As the sample size (n) increases,
a. the sample mean increases.
b. the standard error of the mean increases.
c. the standard error of the mean decreases.
d. the standard deviation of the mean increases.

7. The null hypothesis suggests that
a.   the two samples come from the same distribution.
b.   the two samples come from different distributions.
c.   the two samples come from different but overlapping. distributions.
d.   the two samples come from different but similar distributions

8. Adopting a .05 level of confidence means that you would
a.   accept the null hypothesis if the results could occur 5 times in 100 by chance.
b.   reject the null hypothesis if the results could occur 5 times in 100 by chance.
c.   reject the experimental hypothesis if the results could occur 5 times in 100 by chance.
d.   none of the above

9. An experimental psychologist reports that his statistical test indicates that the difference between his experimental and control group in his latest experiment is highly significant. By this he means that
a.   the difference was highly unlikely to have occurred by chance.
b.   the difference was probably due to chance factors.
c.   the results are very important.
d.   both a and c

10. Rejecting the null hypothesis when it is actually true is
a.   a Type I error.
b.   a Type II error.
c.   a Type III error.
d.   a standard error.
e.   not an error; it's the right thing to do.

11. A Type I error occurs when you:
a.   reject a false null hypothesis.
b.   reject a true null hypothesis.
c.   reject a true experimental hypothesis.
d.   accept a false null hypothesis.

12. In hypothesis testing, both magnitude of the difference and the direction of the difference between two groups are considered in
a.   two-tailed tests.
b.   one-tailed tests.
c.   parametric tests.
d.   nonparametric tests.

13. Parametric tests
a. do not make assumptions about the underlying population parameters.
b. make assumptions about the underlying population parameters.
c. are typically more powerful than nonparametric tests.
d. both b and c

14. Mann-Whitney U-test can only be used for
a. within-subjects designs.
b. between-subjects designs.
c. repeated measures designs.
d. none of the above

True-False

1. A population is a complete set of measurements (or individuals or objects) having some common observable characteristics.
2. The distribution of sample means is not a normal distribution.
3. As the sample size (n) increases, the standard error of the mean decreases, the power of the statistical test increases, and the probability of a Type II error decreases.
4. The null hypothesis maintains that the two samples of scores (experimental and control) come from two different underlying distributions.
5. Adopting a .05 level of confidence means that you would accept the null hypothesis if the obtained difference could occur 5 times in 100 by chance.
6. A Type I error is rejecting the null hypothesis when it is actually true.
7. A liberal statistical test minimizes the probability of making a Type II error.
8. One way to increase the power of a statistical test is to increase the sample size.
9. A two-tailed statistical test considers both the magnitude of the difference and the direction of the differences between two groups.
10. Nonparametric tests are those that make assumptions about the underlying population parameters while parametric tests do not make such assumptions.

11. A simple analysis of variance (ANOVA) uses only one dependent variable whereas a complex or multifactor ANOVA uses more than one dependent variable.
12. In an analysis of variance, the F-ratio under the null hypothesis should equal 0.00.

ANSWERS
Key Term Matching
1. e, f, g, a, b, c, d
2. b, a, f, j, i, h, e, f, g, c, d

Fill-in-the-blank
1. population; (p. 376)

2. sample; (p. 376)
3. normal; (p. 377)
4. standard error, mean; (p. 378)
5. small, increase; (p. 378-379)
6. null, experimental; (p. 380)
7. the experimental and control scores come from the same population; (p. 380)
8. the square root of one less than the sample size; (p. 382)
9. the probability of obtaining a difference as large as this by chance is less than 5 in 100; (p. 383)
10. type I error, alpha; (p. 383)
11. II;; (p. 384)
12. I; (p. 384)
13. power; (p. 384)
14. sample size; (p. 385)
15. one, two;; (p. 386)
16. conservative, powerful; (p. 386)
17. parametric; (p. 387)
18. nonparametric, parametric;; (p. 387)
19. between, within-subject; (p. 387)
20. analysis of variance; (p. 396)
21. between, within; (p. 397)
22. 1.0; (p. 397)
23. multifactor; (p. 403)

Multiple Choice

1. c (p. 375)
2. b (p. 376)
3. a (p. 377)
4. d (p. 378)
5. b (p. 378)
6. c (p. 379)
7. a (p. 380)
8. b (p. 380)
9. a (p. 383)
10. a (p. 383)
11. b (p. 383)
12. a (p. 386)
13. d (p. 387)
14. b (p. 387)

True False

1. T (p. 375)
2. F (p. 377)
3. T (p. 379)
4. F (p. 380)
5. F (p. 380)
6. T (p. 383)
7. T (p. 384)
8. T (p. 384)
9. T (p. 386)
10. F (p. 387)
11. F (p. 396)
12. F (p. 397)

WEB RESOURCES

There are a number of online statistics texts that you can refer to for statistical help.

Introductory Statistics: Concepts, Models, and Applications by David W. Stockburger at Southwest Missouri State University is a good introductory level resource.
http://www.psychstat.smsu.edu/sbk00.htm

Some more advanced concepts are covered in:

PA 765 Statnotes: An Online Textbook by G. David Garson at North Carolina State University
http://www2.chass.ncsu.edu/garson/pa765/statnote.htm

Electronic Statistics Textbook by StatSoft (makers of *Statistica*)
http://www.statsoft.com/textbook.stathome.html

You can also find information about presenting results at the following websites:
Psychology with Style: A Hypertext Writing Guide by Mark Plonksy at the University of Wisconsin – Stevens Point
http://www.uwsp.edu/psych/apa4b.htm

Reporting Common Statistics in APA Format written by Laura Little at the University of Washington
http://depts.washington.edu/psywc/handouts/pdf/stats.pdf

Reporting Statistics in APA Style by Jeffrey Kahn at Illinois State University
http://www.ilstu.edu/~jhkahn/apastats.html

The Online Writing Lab (OWL) at Purdue also has a relevant workshop tutorial:
http://owl.english.purdue.edu/workshops/hypertext/apa/parts/results.html

STATISTICS WORKSHOPS

In addition to the *Research Methods Workshops*, Wadsworth also has a number of online *Statistics Workshops*. A number of these workshops are relevant to this appendix. These workshops include:

- Central Limit Theorem
- Z Scores
- Standard Error
- Tests of Means
- Hypothesis Testing
- Single-Sample t Test

- Independent versus Repeated t Tests
- One-Way ANOVA
- Two-Way ANOVA
- Factorial ANOVA
- Statistical Power
- Chi-Square

You can find these workshops at http://psychology.wadsworth.com/workshops/.